# Music Business Tips For Musicians:

## Make Money from Music, Discover The Music Industry and Explode Your Music Career!

*Tommy Swindali*

# Copyright Notice

No part of this book may be reproduced or transmitted in any form whatsoever, electronic, or mechanical, including photocopying, recording, or by any information storage or retrieval system without expressed written, dated and signed permission from the author. All copyrights are reserved.

# Disclaimer

Reasonable care has been taken to ensure that the information presented in this book is accurate. However, the reader should understand that the information provided does not constitute legal, medical or professional advice of any kind.

No Liability: this product is supplied "as is" and without warranties. All warranties, express or implied, are hereby disclaimed. Use of this product constitutes acceptance of the "No Liability" policy. If you do not agree with this policy, you are not permitted to use or distribute this product.

We shall not be liable for any losses or damages whatsoever (including, without limitation, consequential loss or damage) directly or indirectly arising from the use of this product.

# Can I Ask You a Quick Favor?

If you like this book, I would greatly appreciate if you could leave an honest review

Reviews are very important to us authors, and it only takes a minute to post.

# Download Audio

This book is also available now as an audiobook.
Head over to www.audible.com or
Download on the Audible application

## Are You Ready To Start Earning REAL INCOME With Your Music?

https://www.subscribepage.com/musicbiz

# Other Books by Tommy Swindali

In The Mix: Discover The Secrets to Becoming a Successful DJ
*If you have ever dreamed of being a DJ with people dancing to your music and all whilst having the time of your life then this book will show you how. From the bedroom to the hottest clubs, events and mainstage festivals.* Find Out More

Music Production: The Advanced Guide On How to Produce for Music Producers
*Learn to Produce Music Like a Pro and Take Your Music To a Whole New Level*
Find Out More

Music Production: Everything You Need To Know About Producing Music and Songwriting
*Everything You Need To Know About Making Music In One Place! Grab your chance to own this comprehensive guide by Tommy Swindali. Covering everything you need to know about music production, as well as songwriting.* Find Out More

Music Production: How to Produce Music, The Easy to Read Guide for Music Producers Introduction
*You are about to discover proven steps and strategies from music producers on how to produce music, even if you have zero experience in recording and audio engineering. You will be able to learn everything you need to know in order to make your first single sound just the way you want it.* Find Out More

Songwriting: Apply Proven Methods, Ideas and Exercises to Kickstart or Upgrade Your Songwriting

*Have you ever listened to a song and thought "wow, if only I could write a song like that"? Well, you can now learn all the secrets on how to write beautiful music with this guide to songwriting!* Find Out More

# In This Book You Will Discover

If Your In The Music Business, Read This

Today you need to view yourself through the new rules of the music industry. Those who play by them **will succeed**. Gone are the old days where you would hope to get signed and then become a star *(i.e. everything would be done for you).*

*Do you wonder why other artists are getting breaks and you are not?*

Making it in the music industry isn't about catching that big break anymore. Getting your career off the ground can be a long and scary task. In this cutting-edge book Tommy Swindali maps out everything you need to know and provides you with the tools necessary to get to where you want to be.

*The tools are yours to use, but only if you want it bad enough.*

Find out why you should run your music career like a business. Then allow me to simplify that process and walk you through all the steps that the professionals take. You don't want to be another tired and broke artist forced to get a job you hate. Do yourself a favor. Whether you are an active or aspiring musician, or an aspiring music manager or agent - this book is perfect for you.

In this book you will discover:

1. What to Look for When Making a Deal

2. Understand The Importance of Streaming and Subscription
3. Discover The New Rules of The Music Industry with "360 Degree" Deals
4. Connect With The Right People Who Will Help You to The Next Level
5. Multiply Your Income Forever With Music Licensing
6. How to Get Signed and Have A&Rs Chasing You
7. The Secrets to Using Funding
8. Develop Your Brand and Make a Good First Impression
9. Monetizing Your Music
10. And Much, Much More

So if you want to go somewhere big with your music and/or learn the music business **read on**

## Table of Contents

Introduction ........................................................... 10
  Welcome To The Business ................................. 11
    Turn Up Your Success ..................................... 16
  Turn Your Music into Money .............................. 18
    Mastery ............................................................ 18
    Write and Get Rich ........................................... 19
    Performing Live ............................................... 20
    Engage With Your Fans .................................... 21
    The Entrepreneurial Mindset ............................ 22

Publicity ................................................................ 24
  Brand and Audience Building ............................. 25
    Developing Your Brand .................................... 27
    Make a Good First Impression ......................... 28
    Be Someone .................................................... 30
    Be Unique ........................................................ 32
    Influence ......................................................... 33
  Publicity ............................................................. 33
    Publicity Fees .................................................. 35

Gain Even More Publicity Online ............................ 36
   Social Media .................................................... 37
      Getting Recognition ...................................... 37
      Content ........................................................ 38
      Engage Your Fans ......................................... 40
      Planning For Success .................................... 42
      Paid Content ................................................. 43
      Take Ownership ............................................ 43
   Email list ......................................................... 45
      Collecting Emails .......................................... 46
      Offer Value ................................................... 47
      Quality Content ............................................ 47
      Consider Assets ............................................ 49
      Email Marketing Solutions ............................ 50
      Metrics ......................................................... 50
Getting Signed ..................................................... 53
   Record Labels .................................................. 54
      Getting Singed ............................................. 55
      Perform Live ................................................ 56
      Exposure ..................................................... 56

Prove Your Value ............................................. 57

Independent ..................................................... 59

　　Build Your Empire .......................................... 60

　　How To Start Your Own Label ......................... 61

　　Connections ................................................... 62

Record Label Structure ....................................... 64

　　Artist and Repertoire (A & R) .......................... 64

　　Marketing ...................................................... 65

　　Radio Promotion ............................................ 66

　　Creative Services ........................................... 67

Record Deals .................................................... 69

　　360 Deals ...................................................... 69

　　Joint Venture ................................................. 71

　　Advance ........................................................ 73

Building Your Team ........................................... 76

　　The People .................................................... 77

　　　Booking Agent / Promoter ............................ 78

　　　Agencies and Hybrid Agents ......................... 80

　　　Get Booked ................................................. 81

　　　Public Relations ........................................... 83

- Management ................................................. 83
  - Hiring a Manager ..................................... 85
  - Tour Manager .......................................... 87
  - Artist Manager ........................................ 89
  - Business Manager ..................................... 90
- Lawyers ...................................................... 92
  - Hiring a Lawyer ....................................... 94

# Copyright and Publishing ............................... 95

- Copyright ................................................... 96
  - Registration ........................................... 96
  - Protection ............................................. 97
  - What Copyright Protects ............................. 98
  - Copyright Duration ................................... 99
  - Public Domain Music ................................. 99
- Filing a Trademark ....................................... 103
  - How to Register a Trademark ...................... 104
- Publishing ................................................ 104
  - History of Publishers .............................. 105
  - Attracting a Publisher ............................. 107
  - Performance Income ................................. 107

- Mechanical Royalties ................................... 108
- Synchronization Licenses ............................ 109
- Publishing Contracts ....................................... 111
  - Terms .................................................... 112
  - Territories ............................................. 114
- Getting Paid ..................................................... 116
  - Royalties ................................................... 117
    - Split Sheets ............................................ 118
    - Collection Societies ................................ 119
    - Percentage Splits .................................... 121
  - Streaming Royalties .................................... 125
    - Cost Per Stream ..................................... 127
    - Estimates .............................................. 130
- Licensing and Sampling .................................... 132
  - Licensing an Overview ................................. 133
    - Music Licensing Definition ...................... 134
    - Content Producer .................................... 135
    - Music Libraries ....................................... 135
    - Copyright Owner ..................................... 136
    - Licenses ................................................ 136

- Popular Music ................................................. 138
- Stock Music ..................................................... 138
- Custom Music .................................................. 139
- Video Games ................................................... 140
- Get Connected ................................................ 141
- Sampling ............................................................. 143
  - How To Clear Samples ................................. 144
- Distribution and Merchandising ........................... 146
  - Distribution ..................................................... 147
    - Tunecore .................................................... 148
    - Distrokid .................................................... 149
    - Level Music (Free Distribution) ..................... 152
  - Merchandising ................................................ 154
    - Manufacturing Merchandise ........................ 155
    - Where to Merchandise ................................ 156
    - Price Points ................................................ 157
- Finance ................................................................ 159
  - Finance ........................................................... 160
    - Supporting Yourself .................................... 160
    - Money .......................................................... 162

Tax ................................................................ 162

  Corporation .................................................. 163

  Company Set Up ......................................... 164

  Paying Taxes ............................................... 165

 Financial Statements ......................................... 167

 Crowdfunding ..................................................... 173

  Decide On The Project ................................ 174

  Fan Base ...................................................... 176

  Investors ...................................................... 177

 Sponsorship ....................................................... 180

  How to Get Sponsored ................................ 181

  Offer Value .................................................. 182

Conclusion ............................................................. 185

 Time, Money and Age ....................................... 186

  Time is Running Out .................................... 188

  The Exit ....................................................... 191

# **Introduction**

# **Welcome To The Business**

There is more to a career in music than just making music. People are betting their future on music. Producers, singers, artists, songwriters and creatives. We all spend so much time creating that we automatically assume fortune and fame will be coming our way. Here we stand waiting to be discovered and all we have riding on that is our music. Yes of course it's all good to have that dream of being a superstar and you certainly should. But whilst working towards those creative goals we have got take care of the business side of things.

Whether you are an aspiring artist or music professional looking to do something big in the music business but you don't know where to start well then listen up. I'm going to share with you how the top people in the music business make it, maintain success and grow it. If you look at music as a just a way to express yourself then by all means don't take on my advice here. There's a lot of artists out there who don't want to do it for the business and you know just like playing guitar or writing lyrics and so on. Well that's awesome but if you want a true career out of your music well then at some point you will have to treat it like a business. Otherwise it's just a hobby. Think of your music as being a product and your the boss.

*Realistically if you want to have a career in music then this knowledge is essential.*

Music is ninety percent business and ten percent music. Whether you're an indie artist or signed to a record label you've got to know all about business. As an artist you need to handle your money and for the most part you are going to have to handle a lot of things by yourself. Especially early on.
Breaking into and making a living in the music business has become more and more difficult over the past ten years. People look back to the advent of streaming and Napster as the downfall of the music industry being a profitable way to make a living. However it actually started a little bit before that. In 1996 the Telecommunications Act was signed by President Bill Clinton. Essentially it took what in 1983 was fifty companies owning ninety percent of all the

media and entertainment companies in the United States down to six. Comcast, Walt Disney, 20th Century Fox, Time Warner, CBS and Viacom. At the time of writing that might be even less. They control everything that is seen, heard and read in the United States and have massive worldwide influence.

*Today less people are making the decisions and with more consolidated power.*

Profitability wise the years 1999 and 2000 were the biggest years in the music business. Around 2005 a typical new band would have had a budget of around one hundred and fifty thousand dollars to make their first record. In fact if they were really good, multiple labels would have bid for them and the budget could have been up to two million dollars or more. Although that would have been a recoupable amount of money meaning that it had to be paid back before the band started earning royalties. Not only that but the record would have had to recoup its costs before they even started earning those royalties. Incidentally, some records never recouped money because there was so much money being spent on making them.

Ten to fifteen years ago a typical new band would get thirteen percentage points out of which three points would go to the producer and one point would go to the mixer. A big-time producer that produces hits could get up to a hundred thousand dollars for a track. Plus if they were a writer on it then they would also be earning publishing royalties. Nowadays most bands never make any money from the physical sales of a record. Let's say for example a band spends three hundred thousand dollars on making their first record but in sales they only make back two hundred and fifty thousand dollars. That fifty thousand dollars loss then gets added onto their next bill and the next record ends up costing four hundred thousand dollars. Then for example say they only make two hundred and fifty thousand dollars on that so there's an extra one hundred and fifty thousand dollars, plus the fifty thousand dollars leading to two hundred thousand dollars over spent. Quite the bill. Now at that point the artist or band would probably get dropped but if they didn't then that debt carries on to the next record and so on.

With less records currently being sold it has become more difficult for artists associated with the music business to make a comfortable living. In fact most rely on other supplementary income to stay in the business. Twenty years ago if you were writer you could make a decent income off of earning royalties on album tracks that you had written. Today an album track may be part of a three-way split and the only way to really make it is to have a hit single. Now people always wonder how much money hit singles can bring in for a writer or an artist. Really it's the writers that are the ones who are making the most money out of it. Let's say for example a top five country song will bring in roughly a million dollars and in pop music it'll bring in probably one to three million dollars. That money is split between the writers. If there's three writers and it's three million dollars profit well then everybody gets a million dollars each. Adding to that there's mechanical royalties which is the physical sale of a CD or for a digital download sale. Then there is digital streaming, YouTube, Spotify, Pandora, Apple music and so on. The more watch time you have, the more money they will pay you. Now when you're talking about thirteen billion plays that could equate to about three million dollars profit. If you can become a big artist by having huge hit songs then you can generate millions of subscribers and views.

## **Turn Up Your Success**

Nowadays people that get signed are already successful and record labels act as an amplifier to their success. If somebody has a hit on YouTube, the radio or whatever it may be then record labels will take notice. How can you get to that level of success? The best way is to constantly release new content. If you're not cranking out enough content then your never going to be relevant. Don't be the artist that only drops two singles a year and then gets mad at everybody else because their succeeding. Stop wasting your time on YouTube, Facebook and any other time sinks that don't add value to your business. Your customers don't care about what your political views are or what your opinion is on unrelated subjects.

*They want to know about you as a creator.*

Expose your music to as many people as possible. Ship it out and move on to the next thing when you're promoting. If you have somebody new in your car have your music playing. When you have a good conversation or experience that background music transfers onto the good experience. Promote your music in a non aggressive way, meet people, be nice and then add them on Twitter, Facebook or whatever. Then out of curiosity they might click your link.

*Keep building a relationship with them and they will want to support anything you do because they will like you as a person.*

# **Turn Your Music into Money**

The music industry has a number of different ways for artists and bands to make money. As long as you're growing your fan base and building an audience there are more than enough ways to monetize that.

## **Mastery**

Preparation and mastery are crucial because before you even think about making money from your music you really have to hone your craft. If you are making great music and putting it out there but people still aren't reacting to it then it is probably not yet good enough. The answer is to get back in to the studio, make more music and do that for a long time until it gets better. Start reaching out and find people that can help you become a better songwriter. Find a good local studio, hang out there and help them out. This way you will get to build relationships with the artists, producers and record label staff that come in. Making connections especially local ones will certainly open a lot of doors for your career in music. In addition you will learn valuable skills such as mixing and mastering because will be watching professionals do their thing over and over again. Hopefully they will even let you practice or they may even assign you to client work with so then not only are you there networking you're also learning skills. If all else fails you might be able to use the studio rooms during an open slot. Most likely they will be cool with it since they're not losing anything really and because you've built a relationship with them, they will trust you. Bottom line is that mastering your craft is definitely not going to be easy. However if your passionate and work hard it is obtainable.

## Write and Get Rich

Hone your skills as a writer. Whether you are a pop, rock, country or hip hop artist the writing part is the most valuable. Most artists these days don't write their own songs and therefore are not making as much money as they could be from them. If their songs become huge hits it's the writers that are making all of the money. Not only that but there are so many more avenues to make money from with the writing. You don't have to always be shooting for pop stardom. There are many ways that you can sell your music from ghost producing to jingles. Tons of music libraries exist out there that are paying big money for licensing music to film, TV, libraries and adverts. Maybe you are a producer and you could do syncs or placements for advertisements, productions for other DJs and so on. There is even more money to be made with the royalties that are gained from streaming or selling your original music on Spotify, iTunes, YouTube and so on. Much more on all of that later.

## **Performing Live**

Once you have established yourself somewhat you can start earning additional money through live performances. Artists nowadays make the majority of their money through touring and that translates on a smaller scale also. Maybe you can perform for weddings, corporate gigs and so on. Get started by producing your own events. Present yourself to a venue, pay them and then sell tickets for your show which you can then make a profit off of. Put yourself out there for people to call on you. Really market not just your music but also your performance skills. Once you're able to do that and your music really starts connecting with your audience then your growth should be pretty much organic. Your social media numbers will start to build and you'll eventually start selling your music online which will then eventually lead to opportunities to get booked for even more shows and tours. There you can sell merchandise and find other ways to monetize your fan base.

People have to be willing to pay when they get to that location and this is based on the quality of the experience. The show has to be so good that people want to pay for it again and again. In the audience there will be a lot of people that really rock with you but there will also be a lot of people discovering you for the first time. Be so exciting that even if the person doesn't like your genre then they like your show. It has to be so good that they are excited to come back. You have to get to the point where you can drive people to a destination then sell tickets, merchandise and all these things.

## Engage With Your Fans

Success doesn't come overnight, it might seem like that from the outside. But behind every success are a lot of hours, days, months and years of hard work. You want to be able to put your music out there and have people support you. It's a major accomplishment to be in the studio record, something and put it out there. Have a place where fans, friends and family can listen to you. Today most people are listening to music via streams or downloads online. Getting the music to them is so much easier with do-it-yourself distribution services such as Distrokid and Tunecore. All you need to do is to distribute your own music directly to your fans and then you can pay yourself for the rest of your life.

## **The Entrepreneurial Mindset**

Throughout the process you really have to educate yourself on how the music industry really works. Start thinking more like an entrepreneur and make great music, keep networking, learning and eventually if you can hang in there long enough it will all pay off in the end. Create a brand for yourself then market and promote that brand. That means having all your visuals, graphics and logo on point. That means having all your best videos uploaded to YouTube and making sure they are professional. That means crafting an original sound that you can build your brand around. Not following other trends or other producers but really trying to build your own sound and identity. Once you're able to do all of that you can start the process of promoting and marketing to engage your fan base and expand on your success.

*Let's dive deeper into your journey as an artist.*

# **Publicity**

# **Brand and Audience Building**

To make it in the music business people need to know who you are and that's all a part of awareness building. That's all about making great music, playing amazing shows, marketing, advertising, leveraging other people's fame and associating that with yourself. Create really high quality content consistently then get it out there and market it on mass. Look for people that have a higher following and work on building relationships with them by collaborating in some type of way. Whatever area you choose, do be consistent and of course try to make great music. If you do these things it's going to help increase your potential for success and fortune.

We live in a day and age where the brand is really what sells the concert tickets, gets that social media following, attracts the labels and contracts. In fact the record labels these days don't care much about what your music sounds like. Just look at the people being signed and touring all over the nation. Essentially they all have a strong brand identity. Now depending on where you are in your journey maybe you already have some understanding of how important brand development is to your music career. As a case in point, say that you visit a shoe store. Almost all of the time they will have the brands separated. Big sections of Adidas, Nike, Reebok and so on. The phenomenon of brand loyalty occurs when consumers will go straight to the brand they favor first of all. Listen to the language they use. For example, "I love the way Nike feels" or "I love the way it looks" or maybe "I just love the advertising and feel like I'm part of the tribe". Building that tribe of people that no matter what you put out they believe in you is what it is all about.

Understanding and embracing the fact that you are the brand can be a difficult concept for most artists to adapt to. Maybe you are afraid of being judged or you want to wait for the right moment. The fact is that if you want to be known you have to put yourself out there and get over these hurdles that you set for yourself. Step outside your comfort zone and grow your fan base. If you don't have the cash, spend the time. Don't be the guy who just says, "hey listen to my music" because that's shoving a product in front of somebody else's face without them understanding the brand.

Brand development is the most important thing aside from the music itself. The number one thing that up-and-coming producers, artists, songwriters and creatives can do to improve their business is going to be branding. Branding is the identity of your business. As an artist or band you are a business and that branding is going to be your identity. It's going to be your logo, your website, social media, banners, color schemes, the way you handle yourself online and communicate with people. All of that and more will go into your branding.

## **Developing Your Brand**

Branding is essential and you should always be developing your brand. That can involve researching other brands or influencers in your space and trying to learn from them. Look at the artists that you aspire to be like, take references and plan your business model after them. Analyze their branding, look at their logos and see how they brand themselves. Then consider why they are more successful than you are. Figure out what matters to you at the core. Do you want to be known for your music or do you want to be known for your aesthetic? Maybe it's about some kind of alternative character that you create. What matters to you, your personality as an artist or your music as an artist? Think of people like Travis Scott who created this vivid alter reality. Or Justin Timberlake who is suave and clean cut. Match that with your music. You have to figure out what you're trying to do or create. Even within the music itself, do you want to be known for your melodies or for your lyrics? Maybe you want to be known for the energy that you bring. Start figuring out a few basic things that you feel like matter to you the most. Don't necessarily go towards picking something that you just think sounds good. Define why it is so important to you.

## **Make a Good First Impression**

Branding and publicity do cost money and take time. However the time and money that you do spend on it will more than pay off in the future. Branding can start with a good logo, a website, Facebook ads, social media and graphics. Spend some money and have someone take a couple of good headshots for your profile pictures. Or find a friend that has a more professional camera. There are tons of tutorials on YouTube as far as how to edit with free tools or even use professional ones such as Photoshop or Lightroom and so on. There really is no excuse as to why you can't have a professional-looking profile picture. Start with a consistent professional-looking headshot for all your different social media outlets. Use the same one on all of them whether it's on YouTube, Spotify, Instagram, LinkedIn, you name it. Try to use the same professional looking photo and be consistent in your branding.

Make a good first impression because first impressions mean everything in the way that somebody goes in to listen to your music. If your online presence is great than the visitors first impression is going to influence their opinion of your music. Incidentally it can either make or break you. These things will cost money but they will pay off in the long run since your investing in making a high quality product that will sell well. It's super important to have all of these things in place because every time you are presented on the internet you need to look professional in order to be taken seriously by the people looking to work with you or buy from you. Your website, online presence and social media is the first impression of them seeing your branding and that is their first impression before they even hear your music.

Now realize that your brand is not going to be perfect from day one. Over time you can develop it and change or even reinvent it. There are so many facets to the brand and things that you can choose as your core. It doesn't have to be the traditional oh I'm a lyricist or oh I'm a hype artist or whatever. However you don't want to pick something super broad like positivity or millennials because there are so many different nuances to those broad terms. Understand that when you pick a niche it defines you.

## **Be Someone**

Consistency, dedication, discipline, focus and all of that stuff is the key to actually becoming a somebody. There are tons of people who get drowned in the the pool of mediocrity and inconsistency. Have a posting schedule for all of your social media accounts and online presence. Creating a posting schedule is going to accustom your audience to a routine and keep you away from those distractions of just hanging out on social media all day. Post every single day if you can. It doesn't have to all be on the same channel. One day it can be one Instagram, another day on YouTube and so on.

Give your audience something to look forward to, even if it's not a consistent music post you could give them a peek behind the scenes. Show a little bit of vulnerability, what's behind the curtain. I know so many of us want every single thing to be so polished and that's how we get into this little rut. When you are vulnerable your audience is going to be able to relate to you more. No matter what persona you are trying to show, be yourself because that's where the real audience following is going to come from. People can see right through any fabricated character kind of thing. You have to embrace that vulnerability otherwise it will not work out for you long term.

## **Be Unique**

We are in a very saturated market. Anyone can make a hit song on their laptop and upload it. Set yourself apart from all the rest. That can be done with your logo, website and social media marketing. Even if your music is not quite as good, that first impression is going to make the difference of whether they go with you versus somebody else.

Make sure your branding is solid and you will be able to charge more. Think about all these luxury brands that come around that charge a ridiculous amount of money for the same amount as a lesser known brand. At the end of the day it is the same product and the reason that they are charging more is because their packaging and branding is superior. Consumers buy into that mindset of wow this is a better product that I need and I'm willing to pay more for it. The mind is a powerful thing and it is going to sway people from either going with you or not going with you based on their interpretation of you the first time they see you.

## Influence

At the end of the day people have to be willing to come somewhere or buy something because of you. You are the influencer at the cause of the hype. The only way that happens is when the people get that original awareness. Which is by you creating or doing something that gets them inspired or makes them want to be a part of what you're doing. Tell your story and share it with the world. Connect with people any chance you can and embrace the process.

## Publicity

When you are building your brand and awareness on a larger scale you will want to be working with publicists. In face you will likely be approached by them or they will be part of a record label. PR and publicity is not something an artist necessarily needs right in the beginning stages of their career. Since the demand is less, early on you can do it for yourself until you reach a critical mass. Then to put yourself to the next level you will need to hire a PR or a publicist.

The role of a publicist or a publicity company is to promote any good news of an artist and diminish any bad news. They are the ones pushing the word out whether it's a tour, new album or any other relevant news. Oftentimes they are one of the few people you will ever see listed on an artist website or Facebook page where there is contact information for an artist. They are also the liaison between the artist and any media outlet. This can be TV, printed media, websites and radio. Many time publicists are the gatekeeper between the world and the artists and are responsible for figuring out what's a legit request or a fan. They will take those occasional requests such as artists working with charities or on TV shows and so on.

Publicists are all about building and presenting an artist in the best way. They write or improve on those press releases and biographies of artists to make them sound really good or spin it in a way that gives them an edge. At the same time they are the first people that if an artist is caught in some sort of trouble or and has a rumor going around they are the people that have to get the word out through a press release. In essence they are protecting the artists image. Ultimately they will help out the artists careers for as long as that is.

The majority of big-name record labels have in-house publicists/publicity departments. They will be assigned to specific artists and have been in the industry for a while and therefore understand the different elements of it. This is really useful for getting to the next level since their media contacts will call on them before any individual or independent contractors. Fundamentally they have a well known name that brings more legitimacy to them. If you aren't signed to a label a publicist can help you with promotion as well as set up key promotional events for you.

## Publicity Fees

Publicists usually charge a flat rate fee or a percentage of an artists overall income based on a project they're working on. If they are part of a label then that's factored into the deal you have with that label. Indepently you need to agree on those terms. In some cases they can get a flat fee on the time spent on getting the word out and connecting with different media outlets. Make sure you research on who are good publicists to work with and agree on what the project specifics and budgets are.

*Let's take a look at what it takes to get signed and how record labels work.*

How are you enjoying this book so far? I would love to hear back from you in the reviews section. Please leave a great honest review on Amazon, Thanks!

# **Gain Even More Publicity Online**

# **Social Media**

Making a name for yourself and getting your music heard is undoubtedly a hard task. Social media has given us multiple channels to share our music and gain recognition. Many people have popped and made money because of YouTube, Vine, Snapchat, Instagram and so on that would have never been signed fifteen years ago. Not so long ago artists had to rely on traditional media such as TV and newspapers to promote them. For that to happen you would have required the backing of a major record label. But times are different nowadays and we have our own channels to utilize and reach people through.

## **Getting Recognition**

To get heard, seen and followed you need to be everywhere where potential fans that care about your genre of music are. Join groups on Facebook, forums or reach out to people that have little channels and so on. Start small, one or two steps from where you currently are. Reach out and collaborate with people and then other people that are familiar with them can discover you. Connect with artists in your space and compliment them on their music. Ask them about themselves. Dive in deep and ask where their motivation or inspiration came from. Everybody wants to hang out with somebody that makes them feel good. You need to be that for someone and you need to be that for a hundred, thousand and more people. When you build a community of people they are more likely to share your content because it makes them feel really good. Then you can start adding in things like merchandise and it's completely congruent and as an extension of the music. From there you will see a snowball effect. At the end of the day you want to grow your fan base to either share your music or to make a sustainable living from your music.

## Content

Decide on what you want your social media to say about you and how you can convey that through your content. Most artists are using social media more or less exactly how normal people do. With posts such as, "here's a picture of my pet" or "here's me going on a hike". The issue with that is there is a lack of story and it's not going to attract a lot of new people. Now on the flip side some content is too promotional. Where everything is go download this or go do this. Of course you want your fans to discover your news, tune into your music and all of your other stuff but if that's all you post about then it can get pretty boring. Try to focus twenty percent of your social media content to promote your brand and dedicate the majority eighty percent to content that leads to engagement.

Most of the time it's not that artists don't have the time to make good content it's a lack of ideas. Creativity wins the most attention. Shows like Pop Idol and America's Got Talent always focus the talking point on the people with the story because that is a hook point. People are interested in things like "oh you know, kid came from the streets" or "this kid performed for the Queen" and so on. All of us have a story but most of us just don't think ours is interesting. Just because they didn't have an alcohol addiction or some life drama. Well it doesn't have to be like that.

We are in a saturated market and within that kind of market your content should entertain and hook people in. Social media users have short attention spans. Really try to understand your audience and what drives them. For example if your fan base is based on youths into underground music then you should go with a similar theme. Or if you've got a band that is really about nostalgia and covering old music you may have messages around nostalgic themes. Now be aware of things that might hurt your brand. For example if you're in a death metal band and you're sharing funny stuff then maybe it hurts your brand. The main thing is to be your authentic self and discuss things that you are genuinely passionate about. If all else fails look at the content that is most popular and trending, then reverse engineer why it is so successful. Followers can easily be faked but trying to fake shares or retweets can be much more difficult.

## **Engage Your Fans**

Invent exciting ways to engage your fans. Maybe you have a new album out and want people to share it. Incentivise them and offer things like a free shirt or hat to a lucky follower who shares it. Or offer a reduced price on some merchandise to anyone who joins your mail list. Put your fans to work. When an artist wants to share something with their fan base one of the ways that they're going to get that message out is by getting other people to share that message. For example Beyonce released an album with not a nickel of advertising all she did was a tweet and Instagram post that she has this new surprise album. People felt compelled to share that because they felt like they discovered it.

We share content on because we feel of the way it makes us feel. Maybe it makes us laugh or makes us happy. Essentially we share things for how they make us feel. Everytime you post content think a little bit about that why would somebody share it. you have to keep looking at what is resonating with your metrics and what's getting the most engagement. If you just post something like "hey here's my new track" then that doesn't really work as much as if you post "hey that's my new track it took so long to make and it's so important to me". Make it personal and people will follow. You could do a couple of post per week that are more personal. Then maybe one or two posts per week where you kind of try to sell yourself or your new song.

## **Planning For Success**

Plan out how you can share content across the various social media channels. Adapt over time because the climate online changes rapidly as does what people respond to and so in turn you have to keep adapting. Some things might work well on Instagram, others on Youtube and so on. For a channel like Instagram it's all about the visual side and text is a secondary part. On the other hand with Facebook there is more room to tell a story. Overall you need to plan your content accordingly to each platform. Thinking about it this way allows you to post every day but spread out across the platforms. You can use tools like Hootsuite to plan out your social media schedule. Maybe on Mondays you do a vlog on YouTube, Tuesdays are for a selfie on Instagram, Wednesdays behind the scenes on Facebook, new music on Soundcloud on Thursdays and so on. Get creative and utilize all of your content and platforms. Consistency is the key because then people are hooked into what your doing.

## Paid Content

Paid advertising on social media these days is really powerful. It allows you to boost posts specifically to different regions, age ranges and even on what people engage with and or like. Ultimately you can target your exact audience and raise awareness for your brand. But if you take content that's just bland and you boost then it will get a lot less action than a non boosted interesting post. Therefore we should only promote content based on how it performs first. Even if you have a new album maybe you wait on the advertising side until your fans do the work for you first. There are so many people that just put their music out there and then try to pay to promote it. But if it isn't getting any action already then there is absolutely no value and it becomes a waste of money.

## Take Ownership

Finally, remember that you don't own your Instagram, Facebook or any of the other platforms. Ultimately you don't control whether in two years from now

Facebook's going to take Instagrams reach and kill it. However you can own a blog or a website. This can be a place to house a variety of content that you can keep on growing. That is something you own. Then you can use email marketing to build up and keep your followers engaged.

# **Email list**

Anything that you're looking to put out into the world should make an impact, you want people to talk about it and share it. Whether you are launching an album or just growing your fan-base building an email list is on of the most important things that you can do. Emails might seem a bit too business for most artists who often see business and music as totally separate things and they are but sometimes there are principles in the business world that apply. It's a very effective way of marketing and you really get the most bang for your buck. When you have an email going straight to your fans it represents a direct connection with your audience that no one can take away from you. If you have great intentions and you're sending good material people are going to open up your emails.

There's a lot of specific strategies that you can leverage to make the most out of those efforts. You can get your fans excited about an upcoming song or album that's about to be released. Email marketing is great for this because there's a big buildup through the chain of emails. Then on launch day you just send out a big email blast.

## **Collecting Emails**

Let's say you want to launch a new project and your starting at ground zero without any emails in your list. There are tons of things that we can give our fans in exchange for their email address. Maybe you can offer them access to a music video that no one else seen or early access to your album. if you say like hey I'm gonna be doing a live concert tonight you know through Facebook live or whatever or through some kind of live stream you know and it's it's only for my web viewers right and you say you have to log in or just check in to access my live concert in my live show and I'll email you the link right so put your email address on this page I'll send you the live link and then then you your people are gonna go crazy over a live show that they can watch from their laptop or from their cell phone and they just gave you their email address for you. YouTube put a link in the description put a card in there that sends them back to band camp where they can download that song I just heard for free you've got to be using these different platforms to send that traffic so that you can build your email list.

## Offer Value

These types of specific offers need to appeal to your audience and actually provide value. At the end of the day it comes down to providing value to them. Understand your audience and what kinds of offers would engage their interest. You can utilize advertising campaigns on social media to get more eyes on your content. In those campaigns have links to sign up forms or squeeze pages where they need to offer their email address in return for what you are offering. If you don't have something valuable that cuts through the noise then you're not going to do any good. On the other hand don't give away too much because you need something left to sell at the end of the day.

## Quality Content

Now don't worry too much about the size of your email list because in order to have a successful launch it's more about the quality of content that you're putting out and how engaging it is. Send emails that motivate your fans to go out and download your music or that make them feel good. Avoid sending emails that make you look like spammy. Have empathy for your audience and make them feel important. People don't want to hear about you as much as they want to hear about themselves. So for example if you say something like, 'hey I was thinking about you when I was creating this song and I want to take you on the journey that I was going through. Maybe this is able to lift your spirits, let me know what you think.' Communicating in this way is going to let people know that you care about them. That's something a lot of people miss the mark on when promoting.

Go to email your fans when you want to show them a new t-shirt or a new bracelet or a new you know poster or something that I created. Then there's not a disconnect because it's so in line with your brand. Then you don't have to be worried that people will be angry. You really need to make a connection with people. Without the authenticity and personalization it's just another sales letter. People need to feel a personal connection and that's where having an email list allows us to build very personal relationships. At the end of the day you need an email list to be able to communicate with your fans.

## Consider Assets

Consider what your assets are, what do you have right now that you can afford to give away and still make some money somewhere else down the line. There's different ways you can do this. Train them to open your emails by providing actual value when they do open them. Avoid selling all the time, you've got to give some stuff away for free and give value. In marketing we call it the cookie crumb trail leading them to the big cookie at the end. You can set up a chain of emails that is activated anytime you get a new subscriber. Then for example every day for five days you could send them a new song and then upsell them on merchandise or the album. You want to hook them on the front end and hopefully they'll see what you're all about and love the other things you do.

## Email Marketing Solutions

There are lots of email marketing solutions where you can have a campaign going that's running on autopilot every single day. Mailchimp or Mailerlite are great services. The platform doesn't matter because they all offer very similar features and benefits. You can't do any of this with Gmail, Yahoo or Hotmail you should never be using those for anything professional. In fact it's actually against the spam laws to email people from a free service. Those are limited so you've got to be using a professional service.

## Metrics

A key feature to keep an eye on is your metrics. Let's say you send out an email to one hundred people and three of them open it. That's a three percent open rate and anything that low means something went wrong. You should be seeing forty to fifty percent open rates and sometimes higher. That's something that you want to keep an eye on because if you're sending good emails to a small intimate list. You want to improve that open rate. Focus on the subject line, you've got to have something juicy to get people to open your email. Then once they open it and read it you want them to take that action in your email. Maybe you want them to click on something such as like your Facebook page or download your music. Don't try to do everything at once, learn how to get them to open and be interested in your offer.

Subject lines are the most important element to getting the open rates higher. Good subject lines peak curiosity and are directed at the target audience. Keep it short and sweet once you know in the body of the email just short and sweet enough so that they have time afterwards to clicking and check out what you're offering in yeah I and I can definitely say from experience that curiosity is where it's at if you want to get people to open the email don't tell them what's in the email.

It about building a culture around your music brand so you can start adding in things like merchandise and it's completely congruent and as an extension of the music. From there you will see a snowball effect. At the end of the day you want to grow your fan base to either share your music or to make a sustainable living from your music.

# **Getting Signed**

# **Record Labels**

There are a number of advantages and disadvantages to getting signed to a record label versus going independent. Your probably thinking a record label is going to help you make it really fast. Sad to say but that's not entirely true. The role of a record label is to amplify the success of an artist but if they aren't good or relevant enough then they won't be successful. Every day new artists sign to record labels and the public never hears about them. Sometimes record labels make the wrong choices or sign good artists at the wrong time. Yes, signing with a record label can help to quickly start your career because when you sign they will usually give you an advance of money. This will help you with recording and promotional costs that would otherwise be funded by you. However it does have to be paid back in addition to a share of your profits.

Record labels really are similar to banks in that they give artists loans to make their dreams come true. In addition they will have different services to help you get on television, radio, distribution and build more awareness worldwide. They will have the relationships to pull strings and make things happen. The biggest advantage of signing with a record label is you immediately have the opportunity to go from talking to a few thousand people to millions.

## **Getting Singed**

In order to go the getting signed route you first need some great music. Record labels want to see that there are other people outside of your circle of friends and family that are really into what you're doing. Get your songs are great and then build an audience. Just make sure that there's an audience for your particular style of music. There's nothing worse than having only a few people that are into what you're doing.

Social media gives you a great opportunity to find a worldwide audience. Your music should be engaging with your audience because that's one of the things the labels are going to look at. Make sure that you've got an up-to-date website plus engaging social media content. Have your music ready and available to be heard. The last thing you want is that your music doesn't play or is hard to find.

## **Perform Live**

Performing live will bring more attention. The chances of getting signed will be higher because you will likely be performing to label executives. Another advantage to performing live regularly is that it will help you with testing out new songs. When you can see that a song is working live then it's likely going to be a top seller. So many artists catch the fire and then put it up for download or streaming which leads to massive engagement.

*This will for sure bring attention from record companies.*

## **Exposure**

Get your music out there, start selling and get the buzz going. Build on that buzz whether it be from touring, YouTube videos, or sales. Get the buzz going and then you can reach out to people in the industry.

Take any chance you get to meet them. If there is someone on the radio, go there and meet them. Hand your demos out and get yourself known. Attend conferences and come into contact with these people or through your network. Add them on Twitter, Facebook, Instagram or whatever. Invite them to your shows and actually prove that you're worth it. They need artists who they can develop from the beginning stage.

*Impress them with your ambition and work ethic.*

People will take notice when you show how hard you work and that your fearless. If you left a good impression on them they might click that link in your bio and listen to your music. Then if your music is really good and they like it not only will they support you as a person but they will also support your music.

## Prove Your Value

Going further, prove that buzz works and turns a profit by selling. Prove that you can sell t-shirts, sell out shows, sell songs and get streams. Labels will want to add gasoline on the fire to make even more money. They are there to take what is already successful and make it even more successful. If you already have the buzz and you're already generating income they know that they can make even more money. Realize that record labels are literally the music business and you need to be selling units and making money in order to prove to them that you're capable of making them a return on their investment.

# **Independent**

Social media promotions, music production software and the ease of creating promotional material has opened the floodgates to more music pouring out every year than we could ever consume in a lifetime. We are in a time when it is easy to create a record then release and promote it. Yes the sale of music is declining rapidly and people are becoming conditioned to consume music for free via streaming websites. The overall music industry is struggling to keep up with the ever-changing ways that people discover and connect with music. This is proven by the turmoil which resulted in just three major record labels eating up the rest.

Working with an independent label or independently is becoming more commonplace as a result of the changes. Contrary to going with a major label this route will oftentimes provide you with more of a personalized plan. Where as a major record label will mostly use what they know works and won't necessarily look at the unique elements of your career. Some might say going independent is riskier and harder because you provide money up front to cover costs and carry the burden on your shoulders. However recording is becoming less expensive plus there are so many services catered towards independent artists for promoting, distributing and marketing their music.

## **Build Your Empire**

Now it all does sound like a lot but that's what you have to do in order to build and own your empire. When you go to a label you might think that they will take care of everything for you. But if you research anybody who ever got signed the first thing they will say is that as soon as they got signed was when they started working more. Truthfully it's on you regardless of whether you are signed or independent. You are going to have to work hard no matter what, so why not build your own empire? When you own your music and labels come calling, you are the one who gets to call the shots. Any terms and conditions are decided by you since you are the one offering the most value.

*You will have the leverage to sign if you want to.*

# How To Start Your Own Label

Creating your own independent label is a surefire way to get your music out there. Setting up is quite a lot of work but it's not that hard and if you really want to start your own label there is nothing holding you back. The first step is to first to start your own company and that can be an LLC (Limited Liability Corporation). In some countries it might be a different name. Essentially you are the owner and are reliable for whatever the company is doing. Setting up is really easy it might just take half an hour and then you wait to get your company number. In addition you will need a separate bank account from your private income and spendings to make it easier for the taxes that you have to do at the end of every year. Finally you will need a corporate identity for your label. This includes a logo and cover designs for any releases.

When you're all done with the setup you will need to find the International Standard Recording Code (ISRC) agency for your country in order to apply for a code. This is for labeling your tracks and is embedded into them so that whenever it gets played or released it is traced. Even if it's a remix, edit, shorter version or club version they all need their individual code. After you have the code you can already start looking for a good distributor. There are a lot available with the best two being Tunecore and Distrokid. More on them later. Distributors will basically take your track and distribute them to all stores and streaming services. They also help you to not really promote it but to pitch it to the stores get some good spots on the starting page of these these web stores. Anything released on your label is one hundred percent yours and you can do whatever you want with it.

## **Connections**

The point of whether you need a major record label or not is really a question of what you're willing to give up. Creative freedom is not happening on a record label. Their attitude is going to be it's our money and so it's our choices. The music industry as a whole is still about who you know. Major record labels have powerful connections and countless capital to bank on artists. They can push the go button on transforming the songs you upload into daily radio rotation, interviews and front page articles. Quality control is unfortunately not as much of a priority. Many major labels have signed musicians based on not much more than a viral video or trend. Musicians with talent are going to have to compete.

*Ultimately you need to assess the options and go with what works best for you.*

# **Record Label Structure**

The record label is made up of four departments. This is applicable to both small and large labels. In some cases a label may partner with another label to use their distribution or other services. Right now only three major record companies exist, Universal, Sony and Warner. Everything else that you know from Def Jam to Atlantic and all these record labels that you may be interested in are all under the umbrella of one of those three majors. This might come as a surprise to you that the whole industry is owned by just three record labels. But it has become this way because not too long ago everything was in disarray. People were downloading records and not buying anything. Labels were losing money and started folding, closing, merging or getting purchased. At the end of the slaughter only three remained.

## **Artist and Repertoire (A & R)**

The first department is A&R which stands for Artist and Repertoire. They are the people who actually find new artists and sign them. Back in the day that involved going out to shows to find and meet with artists. Nowadays things are done a bit differently. Many A&R reps still do attend shows but a lot of their scouting is done online. YouTube, SoundCloud and so on are their main sources. In addition to sorting through submissions that come in through the mail. Usually they will have a well-rounded knowledge of the business world as well as the actual music world.

Once an artist is signed to a record label the A&R reps will work on developing their artists sound. They make sure that they are producing great records and even help to choose songs that are going to be released. Oftentimes they will meet with marketing, radio promotion, creative services and be that overall representative of the artist. On a record label many A&R reps are assigned to different artists on their roster and will often work with several artists at a time. Again most of them have been in the industry for a while and have a good understanding of the elements of it.

## Marketing

Marketing or as in some labels also known as Artist Development (AD). When an artist is first signed to a label they will be assigned an AD who will have a team of marketing specialists underneath them. They help to develop the artists image and presentation to the public making sure that it is cohesive and well branded. This covers merchandise such as the music, CDs and any of the artists additional merchandise. Whether it's giving away a signed guitar by that artist, coming up with a poster or designing a contest for the artists and so on. Essentially they are the brains behind all of those promotions and ways of getting the artists name out into the public. Again they are a representative of that specific artist working hand in hand with them whilst also working with radio and other creative services to make sure everything is coherent.

## **Radio Promotion**

These are the people who are actually picking out the songs that will be radio singles for their artists. Not every song on an artists album is going to be a good fit for the radio. Many radio promoters are people who have actually been DJ's or program directors at radio stations deciding which music is going to be played. Therefore they intuitively understand the world of radio. Not only do they pick the songs that are going to be on the radio, they are also calling radio stations and pushing the songs of their artists. Essentially it's very much a sales job and they have to really believe in their artists whilst having a good knowledge of what is being played on different radio stations.

## Creative Services

The final part of a label is the creative services department. Often this is called the art department or image consulting. Essentially they take care of the physical image of an artist whether it's for a CD cover, promo posters and so on. They are the ones who make sure that any image is relevant with the overall branding of their artist. Often they are the ones assisting with music videos and at times they'll even be on set. Many creative service departments include designers taking care of CD covers, merchandise and artist materials making sure again to stay coherent to that overall brand. Creative services work closely with marketing and artist development to coordinate on their artists career.

# **Record Deals**

There are many different types of deals available to a recording artist with the standard being an artist deal. Today these are commonly known as 360 deals.

## **360 Deals**

Back in the day a record labels main income source would be record sales. In the past deals at record labels were normally between twelve to fifteen points for an artist. Deals were based on full-length albums so that really meant you were getting twelve to fifteen percent of whatever the album was selling for in the stores. For the artist what that meant was after they paid back all the money that was spent to record, market and promote the album then they would begin to see their income. Realistically you had to be a superstar to see any profits and so what artists learned was to front-load their deals. In order to offset the fact they would negotiate as large an advance as possible since they probably would never see any royalties. Then that money had to tide them over until performance revenues started to come in.

Profitability wise the music industry peaked in the year 2000. Bands like NSYNC and The Backstreet Boys were selling ten million records each or more. Nowadays that just doesn't happen, if a band or an artist sells a million records it's a miracle. With the advent of digital music things have changed and record labels have found new ways to stay profitable. Previously they could make a great profit with just record sales and in order to cover those losses they implemented 360 deals. They decided that since they were building the fame for an artist to make money in other ways they felt that they were justified to also take a percentage of profits from those other ways.

Nowadays almost all artists will sign a 360 deal. Essentially it takes a percentage of the artists live performance money, publishing, record royalties, merchandise and everything else that they make money from in music. What that means is that the label is going to take half of almost everything except for on their show money where they might do like a 70/30 split with seventy percent to the artist and thirty percent to the label. The record label will agree to take a percentage of all that for the duration of a contract. The more income that you have as an artist the more leverage you're going to have in negotiating a deal. When an artist signs a deal with a label they need to be aware of what will be included in the 360 deal. Otherwise they could just sign away a circle around themself that gives the label everything.

## Joint Venture

The next deal up from a 360 deal is a joint venture and that's where maybe you have your own label and you do a deal with another label. There's different ways that you can do that deal and that would depend on how successful the artists on your label are. Let's say your label put out artist A who did pretty well and then put out artist B and they did really well which then caught the attention of other labels. The record labels might then offer you anywhere from eighteen points for each artist or a straight split. That could be 25/75 meaning they get seventy five percent and you get twenty five percent. Or it might be 50/50, it just depends on what your bringing to the table. In a joint venture it's rarely more in your favor. Typically in a joint venture each party brings something to the table. For example, maybe your team takes care of social media, video and publicity. Whilst the other team takes care of funding. Independent artists can also do this type of deal but it's very rare that an independent artist has the money to get to this level.

The best deal would be to do a straight distribution deal. That's an 80/20 split with the artist or independent record label keeping eighty percent of the income and the distributor keeping twenty percent. Almost anyone that owns a real business and has some funding to market and promote their artists (including the artist) can do this type of deal. In addition it is possible to do this deal independently through distributors like Tunecore and Distrokid. You just pay a flat fee per single, album or per year. More on that later.

It's really up to you whether you want to sign an artist deal, joint venture or do a straight distribution deal. Just understand that the decision comes with some weight. If you're going to get a distribution deal for your company you're going to need to have the money to market and promote. You're going to have to hire a publicist, marketing people, radio people, video people, social media people and a team of people to help you get to the next level. Finding the funds to do that would be your responsibility. In that regard either you need to get a business plan put together and find an investor or you need to borrow the money.

Remember to take all of this into consideration because there's a very good chance that you could waste a ton of money on people that say they can do the job but can't.

## **Advance**

The term advance is possibly the most misunderstood term in the music industry. When you sign a record deal they will usually advance you some money at the start. Typically if you're a brand-new writer you're going to require an advance at the beginning of a contract period. Normally the record label will want to spread the advance with some at the beginning of the period to record your project and then release some at the end once you have fulfilled your commitment. If the label pays you advances later on you allow them to recoup the money from your royalty shares. Therefore to a great degree the amount of money that they advance is risk money because you may never write a song that produces anything. However 360 deals can serve to protect the label.

Any advance should be spent wisely because it might take a while for any profits to come. There is a fine line between taking too much and taking too little. On the one hand you want enough to cover your expenses whilst you build your brand without being profitable. But on the other hand you don't want to take so much that you're in debt forever. The bigger the advance the less you can negotiate the royalty share. Long term that's much more important because those royalty statements are going to come in for probably the next twenty years or more.

# Building Your Team

# **The People**

Every single successful band or artist has an established team behind them. They will help take you from an unknown struggling artist to the one with success, fame and fortune. There are certain people that you will need in your team to make that happen. At the start of your career you don't necessarily need to hire all these people and start immediately paying monthly for PR and a management team. Look at your budget, how much are you making and how much can you afford to invest? If you have enough money to afford a PR guy but can't afford a manager yet that's okay just start with the PR guy and slowly over time start adding extra people. It all depends on if you have a system that's in place to pay for all these things and grow. If you can pay for all your crew and have some money left over then that's a good system. Starting out your going to need a team that takes care of your shows so you can start generating a buzz whilst getting paid. Then you can expand into more managerial roles.

Let's take a look at some of those people you are going to need.

## **Booking Agent / Promoter**

Shows are going to help you build a profile, become a better performer and get paid. First start out with promoters but just enough get to know your local scene. Get to know your local promoters then work on getting booking agents, PR guys and all this stuff. There are different ways to book shows depending on the level that you are at in your career. You can either work with a booking agent, agency or an independent contractor. Alternatively you can even do self booking and in the very beginning you might need to do that. There is a lot of a lot of rejection in self booking because if you don't have that well-established company name behind you many venues won't take you seriously. It's a very difficult world but there are many artists out there that are doing very well with self booking. It's all based on the drive, dedication and the time you put into it. Build those relationships with venues, bookers and set yourself apart from the millions of booking inquiries they receive daily.

Well-established artists don't really have to scope out shows. People will often be requesting to book them through a booking agency. There are a few agencies and booking agents working with established venues that represent really big name artists. They have worked in the industry for many years and know what places are going to help advance their artists career. This involves going to each venue and making sure that everything is prepared for the shows. Booking agents are kind of like the managers or protectors of all things tour related. They might be handling the cheques, making sure the artists show up, booking plane tickets, hotels or things of that nature. Most of the time whoever's doing the booking is going to be handling all those aspects and of course negotiating the deal.

Their income is based on the profit of a show so obviously they want you to have the best show experience. Typically they take a percentage either off of the shows individually or off of an overall tour. Each one will have different terms and ways that they like to structure deals. Just shop around for rates and figure out which ones work for you. The industry standard is a twenty percent fee for agencies. This will usually be put on the top of the artists fee. Independent contractor are a more affordable option and may only take ten percent or even less.

## **Agencies and Hybrid Agents**

There are two types of booking agents. Agencies which are big booking companies usually working nationwide or hybrid booking agents who specialize in smaller regions. Hybrid agents will have a region that they have perfected and done a lot of business in. For the most part they are going to be very localized and so you can't do a big national tours with them. Although what some artists will do is to find hybrid agents in different regions and make up a nationwide or even worldwide tour through combining them. Now in the early stages this is more likely and it is of course going to take up more time. Later on you are more likely to work with global agencies. However they will want to see that you have some success and a good track record worth their time and investment. A booking agent may represent a company that does corporate functions or an organization that has a lot of festivals and events. Then their job is to meet the needs of the people that are hiring them. In that regard they have to be very particular with what type of acts they bring into a venue.

## **Get Booked**

In order to attract a booking agent you need to make sure that you're doing everything it takes to start creating revenue because a booking agent is going to want someone that's generating value. There is no point them putting you in the building if you can't bring people in there. The number one easiest way to find a booking agent is through networking. Unfortunately most of us are not great networkers but if you know someone who knows someone or if you know a booking agent get in touch. Go to events where booking agents maybe such as conferences and things of that nature. Booking agents are also often at major venues trying to figure out what's hot.

*Nothing beats word-of-mouth.*

Booking agents have to frequent venues that are popular and where all the next new hot talent is currently performing at. If you've never performed there then you're not in that conversation. There's no point in going out there and doing all of this work in a space where nobody's watching you unless you're just practicing and perfecting your craft. You want people to say you do amazing shows and things that bring excitement to you. These guys want to know that you can bring in the cash. Keep a really good record of your sales, merchandise sales and fan base statistics. Websites like soundcloud allow you to check all sorts of data and see where your fans are actually playing your music from. Utilize that data and use that as leverage to get paid shows in different areas or to attract a booking agent. You may not know the venues out there but a booking agent that's well versed is going to know who to talk to. If you can show them for example, we're getting over two thousand people listening to our stuff in Miami or we got a thousand people in Nevada then this can create an opportunity to drive revenue into both of your pockets.

Then it can pretty much be determined that you can pull people into a venue.

## Public Relations

Public relations (PR) also known as publicists. Essentially they deal with the press. This involves getting their artists interviews with blogs, internet radio, radio stations and whatever it is. They try to get their artists seen in the public as much as possible. They want them to be in the spotlight and will help to achieve all those things. If there is a media scandal around one of their artists then they will be the ones speaking on their behalf. It is their duty to protect the image of their artists. Public relations get paid on a monthly basis and that can be advantageous. However make sure you're getting your money's worth. More on that later in the publicity chapter.

## Management

Management exists to take over the burden of dealing with an artists business matters. Artists need to be focused on writing songs, recording, touring and doing all the things that artists do. There is barely an artist out there that is competent to deal with the sort of business issues that need to be dealt with on behalf of them. It is arguable that you could be well represented by just a lawyer and an accountant. Then on that basis you possibly don't need a manager at all. However a good management team will take you to places that you won't be able to go to on your own. They will have connections with record companies, publishers, promoters, agents and all the various people required for a having successful career.

Essentially it is their responsibility to make sure that whatever they do is to further push their artists career to the next level. It's very grueling work and the risk of being rejected is huge. Most artists don't like to be rejected but the manager will take those rejections gracefully and probably never even tell the artist. In addition they will have the authority to be a legal representative for you. They can sign checks for you, receive money for you, sue for you, collect money for you and do all of these things on your behalf. Pretty much they take care of all the business in the background for their artists.

## Hiring a Manager

Before hiring any manager you first have to figure out what you're trying to achieve. Questions will help you discern what type of manager you need or if you even need one to begin with. Are you trying to be a mainstream artist? Do you want more shows? Are you trying to make lots of money? The next thing you have to understand is what a manager does. A lot of people assume a manager takes a nobody and turns them into a somebody. Some managers may have that capability but for the most part if you have no sales or buzz going then there's nothing for them to do and quite frankly you are wasting their time. Next you have to ask yourself can you really afford a manager? Understand that a manager will be paid on a commission basis. They're going to take anywhere from fifteen to thirty percent of any revenue that they help you to generate. If you're not bringing a good income to the table then it is of no benefit to them or you.

Managers can be found by word of mouth and through generating a buzz. Now let's assume you found the manager you want to get into a deal with. They are not hiring you, you are hiring them to guide, counsel and advise you. Technically it's not an employment contract but it's what the law calls a "contract for services". The whip hand by and large in this negotiation is going to be held by the manager. Every contract has a term. If you're a new act normally management will want two years with the option for more at the end. During the term of this contract you cannot be managed by anybody else unless you terminate it legally. On their side usually it's not an exclusive relationship which means that they will not be only working with you. There are plenty of managers out there who manage multiple artists at a time and in a way that helps because they know the things to take from one artists success and apply that to you.

There are so many horror stories of getting into a contract with the wrong manager so make sure you are careful before signing up. Getting out of a contract with a manager will usually require you having to give them thirty days notice. If your paying someone you want to make sure that they will be getting you in front of big names. Make sure that they are helping you look very professional. At the end of the day management is there to represent and advise you in order to get you to the next level of your music career. They can make or break artists.

In an artist career there will be three different managers, tour manager, artist manager and a business manager.

## Tour Manager

The first manager an artist will oftentimes have in their career is a tour manager. Also known as road managers they are in charge of planning ahead before their artists go out on the road. Technically that is called advancing shows which requires confirming and making sure everything's ready for the show. Oftentimes tour managers will have a list of shows that an artist is going to be playing at along with contacts for the venues. They will call up those contacts and make sure that everything is prepared in advance for the show. This can include any little detail that the artists might need to know about that show or venue. Therefore the tour manager really needs to make sure ahead of time that the tour runs as smoothly as possible. In addition oftentimes when an artist is just starting out independently they will be the ones that are in charge of routing tours or even helping with some bookings.

A tour manager doesn't have to come from a big agency. It can just be a friend that knows the business. Just make sure you find someone who can really be on your side because they are the ones who are going to negotiate fees and make sure you get paid. No-name artists can have a tour manager and big name artists can have a tour manager. The tour manager's job is very difficult, they have to be dynamic, love to travel and be great with people. Essentially they are the ones who will take care of the artists whilst they are on tour. Their duties can be anything from driving the van to making sure the artist is there on time for sound checks and for the show. Once that artist becomes more popular enough they will have their own entourage with people taking care of smaller things. Tour managers typically make a percentage off of shows and merchandise sold at the shows for a duration of contract.

## Artist Manager

Artist managers often come into play once an artist has built a pretty good fan base and are showing signs that they are going to be successful and ultimately get signed. In some cases artist managers may also help artists to get signed. Essentially they are the right-hand man or woman of an artist and instigate the liaison between every element of their career.

There are artists management companies and then there are independently contracted managers. Day to day they make sure that the artist knows where they need to be, at what time and what they need to be doing. Again they are going to be super close with the artists so you need to get along with them. Those artists are going to call them in the middle tonight when their vans break down or whenever there is a problem and they don't know what to do. Also they are the promoter that represents the artist in the music community whether it's pushing their music to a label saying "hey I have this artist you need to check out". Or they can be promoting online. Sometimes artists don't control their social media and these managers are the ones running that for them. Ultimately they are the kind of the person who is in charge of the career growth of the artist. Many of them will have been in the industry for a long time and understand what works and what doesn't. Always work with a manager who's been in the industry for a while and not one who's just starting off because you want somebody who has established contacts.

Artist managers make a percentage off of every element of an artist's career whether it comes to merchandise, music sales, shows and so on. Oftentimes it is ten to fifteen percent. Really good managers can make up to twenty percent. Many times they take on clients for free at first because they believe they're going to be successful and in turn make them a lot of money.

## Business Manager

The business manager takes care of all money related matters and oftentimes they are accountants who have worked in the music industry before. Money is important and it requires designation and expertise. Business managers know money really well and they know how to help artists save. If artists are making poor financial decisions then it's not going to provide them with a lot of sustainability. Oftentimes they come in as consultants on a flat fee or work for an artist on a specific project.

# **Lawyers**

Independent record company's, major record companies and any other companies that are involved in the music business all use lawyers. For an artist, when they hit a peak in their career and it starts to become profitable they will require lawyers. Anytime music is being used commercially there's going to be a lawyer on both sides of the transaction trying to protect their party's interest. As a smart business model it pays to have any contracts that are provided to you reviewed by a lawyer to make sure that you're not signing up for something you don't want.

Even a very simple deal ought to be run by a lawyer. Some of the biggest mistakes have been made in the music business by people who at the beginning of their careers signed long-term deals where they were tied up for important rights. People like Billy Joel, Bruce Springsteen and Michael Jackson had contracts that caused some difficulties. A lot of times if they'd had a lawyer review it they might have avoided some of these problems.

Lawyers have detailed knowledge about all the different deals with all the different companies and all the different aspects of their clients. Music lawyers often know all the record companies and can help get somebody heard much faster or even get involved in helping artists find deals. Then they can facilitate deals for major artists that may be looking for a specific kind of deal or if they are stuck between contracts. They will help go to the different labels to structure deals and negotiate. Unlike managers or agents who are limited to the number of people they can handle lawyers can take on more.

Most of the lawyers time is spent either drafting, negotiating or dealing with various contracts. The majority of this is done via email and phone. Primarily their clients are artists but they also work with people who are songwriters which may or may not be the artist. In other words the person who writes the song may not be the one who sings it. Some lawyers also work with producers who are the people that are behind the scenes. They make sure that their client gets what it is that they're trying to accomplish in their lives and gets it with the least amount of of legal hassles whilst making sure they are protected.

## **Hiring a Lawyer**

The best way to find a lawyer is by doing your research, finding out some names and then simply contacting them. Becoming a music lawyer requires going to the best law school possible and then joining a private practice that specializes in music law so you can learn on the job. Alternatively if you want to be on the company side then you can join a record company or a publishing company that would develop and train you.

Lawyers usually work for an agreed flat fee for a term or project. Fees can be quite high but again they are worth it if your playing at a high level. If you can't afford to pay a lawyer there's sites like Legal Shield where you can pay twenty dollars a month for legal advice. Forward it over for them to see if there's anything that may be a little bit disadvantageous or maybe puts you in a bad position. Twenty dollars a month is way worth the expense compared to losing the rights to your masters and having to sue your label. This kind of thing happens frequently and you need to use precaution when dealing with record labels.

How are you enjoying this book so far? I would love to hear back from you in the reviews section. Please leave a great honest review on Amazon, Thanks!

## Copyright and Publishing

# **Copyright**

Copyright is the proof of ownership of an intellectual property. In our case that would be a song. Copyright goes on file as the proof of ownership along with the date that you register. If someone else steals a part of the song or all of it then this is the proof that you are the owner.

Technically you own the copyright to a song as soon as you write it. The moment you create something it only needs to have two things to be eligible as your own. First it needs to be original which means and then it has to have some element of creativity. The Supreme Court refers to this a "Modicum of Creativity".

## **Registration**

Copyright registration can be done with the Copyright Office. The process is very straightforward, you can either upload your song to their website or via mail. At the time of writing, uploading a song costs fifty five dollars whilst mailing it costs eighty five dollars.

Previously a lot of artists on a budget would put their music on a CD inside an envelope with the lyrics typed out. Then they would seal it with their name signed across the seal and mail it to themselves. The postmark would prove the date of the song and the signature shows that it has not been opened. Although this method does prove it's your song, it doesn't allow you the legal right to sue for damages. Because if somebody steals your song you absolutely want to sue for damages. Filing copyrights will protect you in court and you will be relieved that you registered your song because now you can sue somebody for stealing it.

## **Protection**

If you are releasing music to the public and making money with that music then you need to individually copyright your songs. Suppose you are recording songs and you're not quite sure which ones you will use commercially yet then I would suggest that you bundle them together. If you've got ten songs with one producer and five songs with another producer then you will need to do bulk copyrights. Ten will have the same writer and producer and then the five others will have another writer and that different producer. It can be expensive if you have to register multiple songs but if you do it as a body of work or an album then you can cut down on the costs.

## **What Copyright Protects**

It's important to know what copyright does protect. With respect to music you'll find very little in there. The word melody occurs once but there's no mention of rhythm, note, tempo, chord progression or any of that. You also can't predict what could constitute copyright infringement

Copyright protects your expression but it does not protect an idea. For example if you had an idea to write a song about someone you broke up with. Then someone who did this before thinks you're copying their music or their expression well then you're not because by default this is just a basic kind of idea.

For creators copyright gives exclusive rights to exclude other people from doing anything with their music. The first right is that no one else can copy the work, only you can. The second right is the right to create derivative works. In other words if you write a song only you can license it for other purposes such as TV or movies. The third right is the right to perform it publicly. As the creator you have the right to stop your song from being performed. Another right is to stop public display such as lyrics on shirts. Finally you can prevent anyone from digital audio transmission without your permission on sites such as Spotify.

## Copyright Duration

The process of copyrighting takes about six months although it's actually copyrighted the minute you upload it. The period of copyright for a song is the life of the author or if more than one author the last of the author's to die, plus seventy years.

## Public Domain Music

Public domain music is in essence music that belongs to everyone. Let's break down that phrase, public means open to all people and domain is an ownership of space or things. Think about a sidewalk, any sidewalk on any public street belongs to everyone and so it is in the public domain. Public domain music is music that belongs to everyone. But how does a piece of music get to be in the public domain? There are a few ways, actually the first is that the copyright for the song expires. Copyright law has changed a lot since the first Copyright Act was passed in the US in 1790. Now it takes at least seventy years for the copyright to expire on a piece of music. Anything recorded before 1923 is in the public domain.

Another way music becomes public domain is if the author releases it to the public. This is done by the author simply creating a statement that they will release all the rights to their work. Then the music can be used by anyone and the original composer of that music has no control over how other people can use the music.

Finally music or audio recording can be public domain if it was created for a government project. The US government is an extremely large publisher of content and as long as the content was created by government officials or employees as a part of their official duties they are by law non copyrightable. However you have to be careful when trying to find music on government sites. A lot of music in the Library of Congress collections are recordings of artists who are not government employees. Therefore many of these works may still be under the copyright of the composer. Keep that in mind in your search for public domain music.

In general if a song is in the public domain it's only the original version that can be used without permission. However if the song is used in another production then that particular production can be copyrighted. As an example if a producer uses some public domain music in a remix then that remix can then be copyrighted. This is because the original public domain music has been altered enough to be a new original song. This goes for new arrangements of old pieces of music as well. Christmas music is a good example of this. Silent night' is a very old Christmas song and any rights on the song have long since expired so it's in the public domain. But when contemporary artists record their own version of the song on holiday albums they can then copyright the new arrangement of it. However that original public domain music is still available for anyone to use.

# **Filing a Trademark**

Copyright unfortunately does not apply to a name or title. But a trademark can help to secure that name. When you start establishing a name for yourself and are gaining a huge fan base it's important to make sure you have the rights to your name. Otherwise later on down the line you could get sued and have the right to use it taken away. That's going to lose a lot of fans. Case in point Dash Berlin were a production and live DJ group consisting of three members. Two producers and one front man, with Jeffrey Suitrous as the face and DJ of the group. After a long and massively successful history, the two producers decided that they no longer wanted Suitrous to use the Dash Berlin name and filed a lawsuit against him. In effect this stopped him from performing under that name. Dash Berlin gained a huge following and massive brand during their working years. Jeffrey Suitrous has now been faced with the dilemma of building a new brand and retargeting those original Dash Berlin fans. Registering a trademark can help circumvent these kind of issues.

# How to Register a Trademark

Registering a trademark is fairly easy and to file one these days and you don't even need a lawyer. You can do it yourself by going to https://www.uspto.gov where they have an application. First thing you need to do is search their database to make sure that someone else is not using that name. If they are then obviously you will get rejected. But if it's all clear you can file online. They will ask you questions of exactly what the name is going to be used for. What kind of services is it going to be used for and some other simple questions.

*The process costs around around three hundred dollars and takes approximately six months.*

# Publishing

Music publishing is a way for artists to earn some decent extra money. If you're a writer but you haven't yet got a recording contract or a way of getting your recordings to the public a publisher will help. It's in their interest to do so because the more income that they can generate from your songs that they are looking after for you the better. They're going to ensure that you make as much money out of your songs as possible because they will get a share of it

## **History of Publishers**

Historically publishers came up at around the late 19th century when sheet music was becoming more popular. Essentially what they did was hold the rights to the sheet music and then sell it to members of the public. As you can imagine it was a pretty small fry business in those days and that didn't change greatly until the advent of sound recordings. When records started selling in vast quantities the publishing industry became more established.

From the mid-1950s to the mid 1960s there were two classes of people in the music industry. There were performers who rarely if ever wrote their own material and there were songwriters who rarely if ever recorded their own material. Most of your favorite artists only perform or record the composition you hear on their album. However that is not to say all artists don't write a song. A performer is basically anyone who's licensed a song in order to publicly perform it. The performer doesn't have control of the song because it's controlled by the songwriter or the publisher. For example Rihanna or Beyoncé are considered as performers. They have been known to write a song from time to time but mostly they purchase the rights to songs. Most of the big name artists will negotiate terms to buy a song from a ghostwriter only if they're getting writing credit as well or on the song as a writer. This allows them now to acquire the songwriters royalties or split those royalties with the original writer.

Now the question arises, why would the writer even think about giving away the rights to a song? Well if it's a famous performer working with them it will likely make a writer's career more successful than it probably already is. Then it is a win-win for the writer and artist since also it gives the illusion that the artist co-wrote the song.

The business of a publisher is to take songs written by their writer clients and find recording artists who would record the song to in turn generate an income from it. Historically their primary motivation in those days was to collect money and increase the ways of earning money from that song particularly by getting other people to record it. They also would to negotiate with film, TV and entertainment companies to acquire synchronization licenses.

## Attracting a Publisher

If you have songs that sound like they can generate income meaning they sound like they could be on the radio then that's going to entice a publisher to want to work with you. I highly suggest you make at least ten current sounding radio charting songs. If you do that it's more about linking up with good publishing companies who can basically bring you in and vouch that you are a person who can write songs.

*There are a three main sources of income in publishing.*

## Performance Income

Performance income which is the income that anybody performing your song in public has to pay in order to be able to perform your song in public. That applies to bars, clubs, shops, stadiums, concert halls and any public place. The big money there is in broadcast income because every time a song is played on the radio or on TV it counts as a public performance. Performance societies collect that income from various sources. In the USA that is ASCAP, SESAC and SoundExchange. In the UK it is the Performance Rights Society (PRS).

## Mechanical Royalties

The second biggest publishing income is called mechanical royalties. The terminology goes back to pre disc recordings where music was stored on mechanical devices and from that the name stuck. Essentially it is the right to mechanically copy a song onto a sound recording. This royalty is paid by anyone who makes sound recordings and distributes them out into the world. This is accountable for every recording or every copy of a recording that is made. With downloads and streams its an amount per play or stream. The loss of sales of CD and other forms of hard copy recordings has yet to be matched by the amount of money that record companies are earning from digital music. Mainly because a vast quantity of those downloading operations are free ripoffs that don't pay royalties to anybody. Although that income has declined, performance income has marched up steadily.

Mechanical royalties are collected in the USA by the Mechanical Copyright Protection Society (MCPS). It is a publisher owned organization so all of the receipts that it gets are paid to its publisher members. The publisher then pays the artists their share which is usually seventy five percent with twenty five percent retained by the publisher.

## **Synchronization Licenses**

The third source of publishing income is what are called sync / synchronization licenses. These are licenses granted by the publisher or the owner of the copyright permission to use a song with movies or TV. Anytime there's a combination of sound and visual it requires a license from the owner of the copyright and that is called a sync license. Synchronization income is building and is up about fifteen percent in the last ten years. The potential is huge because there's a vast amount of broadcasting and programs out there. Nearly all television channels in all countries broadcast twenty four hours a day. That requires filling a lot of programs that feature music.

# **Publishing Contracts**

Most artists these days have publishing contracts. If an artist is writing their own songs they can sign up for publishing deals on each song that they write. Those can be done with in-house publishing deals at a label or with standalone publishers. Years ago a publisher would first of all take an assignment of copyright. Which meant that from the moment you signed up to a publisher you no longer owned your own songs. Anything that you wrote during the term of this publishing agreement would belong to the publisher for the whole life of copyright and all you got was a share of the income generated by the songs written by you during that contract. That used to be a fifty fifty split between the writer and the publisher.

These days a typical songwriter agreement looks different. First of all no writer ever gives the publishing company a life of copyright assignment. It just doesn't happen anymore. Very few publishers would have the tenacity to ask for that. These days instead of assigning for life of copyright you assign for a fixed term. During which the publishing company gets rights to the songs. Let's say for argument's sake it's a five-year term contract with options for five or ten years extra. In total a period of maybe ten to fifteen years at the end of which the publishers rights have expired and the song becomes yours all over again.

During the period of that assignment all rights in the song are assigned to the publisher. This means there is no limitation of what they can or cannot do with those songs unless you put into the contract that you can't do the following things without previous written consent. For example that could be things such as not using the music in films or in conjunction with political things, in connection with tobacco products or alcohol products and so on.

## **Terms**

All publishing deals are exclusive for a term during which you can only write for a particular publisher. Generally that is expressed as an initial period with options always in the publishers favor. That exploitation period in the music business incidentally is called the retention period. The term of the contract generally means the exclusivity period and the retention period is the period after the end of the exclusivity period that the publisher still has rights. But not for anything that's written during that exploitation period, only for the songs that were written during the exclusivity period.

For simplicity sake say its a five-year term. Therefore everything you write during that term the publisher gets to publish. You can't go anywhere else during that time and you will have signed to a writing commitment. The publisher will likely want you to write X amount of songs during the course of each contract period and this contract period will finish once you've satisfied that obligation. The songs the publisher receives are those written during the exclusivity period and they have the right to exploit those songs for that period plus during any extension. The typical commitment is an albums worth of material written, recorded and released. If you don't write that within the contract period then the period continues until you do. However that doesn't happen very often because writers don't dry up as frequently as you might think. Sometimes they get into a dispute with the publishers and don't want to actually deliver them any more material but that's a different story.

## **Territories**

If you are a new songwriter you're probably going to do a worldwide deal. At the start you wont need to do different deals with different publishers because it's difficult enough to figure out what one publisher is doing for you let alone publishers in different territories. But as you become more sophisticated and successful you will come to realise that there are very few publishing companies that are great in all of the major territories. Different publishing companies are better in different territories so at some point you might decide to break up the world into more manageable chunks. Typically you would want a publisher in the UK, Europe, North North America, Canada, South America and Asia. I wouldn't discourage you from doing that. However you need to be quite successful in order to be able to have good enough accountants and lawyers to do the deals for you and interpret the various royalty statements.

# **Getting Paid**

# **Royalties**

Now when you decided to become a producer or artist you made a decision to do something you have a passion for. I constantly reiterate the importance of understanding that this is a business and businesses are created to make money. In order to make money you must know where your income streams will be coming from and none are more important than your royalties.

A royalty is a payment made to the legal owner of a work of intellectual property by those who want to make use of it for the purpose of generating revenue. In most cases royalties are designed to compensate the owner of the music. This is usually the songwriter who is the person or people who write the lyrics and melody for a song. The term "songwriter" originates from when you had to write music out on a piece of paper. From a licensing standpoint a producer is also considered a songwriter

Songwriters and publishers are the ones who earn most royalties. Producers also do get paid a percentage of the artists royalties. For instance an artist might agree to pay the producer a percentage of every royalty. That is generally a part of the producers compensation. Typically a producer will negotiate a percentage of the retail sales of an album they produced as well as a cash advance on those royalties. Advances can range anywhere from three to fifteen thousand per master and sometimes even higher depending on the producer.

## **Split Sheets**

When it comes to making sure you receive royalties the first thing that must be done is a split sheet which defines who did what on the record. Now this is very important because if for any reason there's ever an action called on the record where people are saying okay this person didn't get paid. The split sheet cuts all that noise and clearly shows who did what along with the signatures.

As an example, if there were five producers then it must state who they were and how much they contributed. Let's say those five producers all equally contributed then there's ten percent each because the record is conceptually broken up into two halves. Fifty percent to the writer and fifty percent to the producer. The more producers or writers, the more royalties get divided.

If your signed to a record label for every record you sell your record company is required to pay you money otherwise known as a mechanical royalty. Mechanical royalties were established by the US government. If you're the songwriter the record company is required to pay you a mechanical royalty of nine point one cents for every record that they sell. So if someone records your song, then for every album they make the record company owes you nine point one cents. Sell a million records and times nine point one cents equals ninety one thousand dollars in your pocket.

## Collection Societies

When you are the owner of a copyright it allows you certain rights. One of those is the right to perform your music in public. Radio, television, at a bar, nightclub or even an elevator all count as a public performance and as the copyright owner you can stop them from using your songs. However if you want to monetize this you can grant them a license in exchange for a fee. A performing rights organization is an entity that licenses the public performance of musical works on behalf of the copyright owners. In America and Canada those are ASCAP and BMI. In England there's the Performing Rights Society (PRS). There is another called SESAC but you can't just join SESEC you have to be interviewed by them and they have to accept you. They are the smallest of the three but ASCAP and BMI are free to join. ASCAP costs twenty five dollars to join as a songwriter alright so it's cheap to lifetime. Then you will register your songs with them. Wherever you are based you need to get your songs registered with one just in case it does start getting played out because that's how they will track it and pay you. On the whole they are all really reputable companies.

Many publishing companies account in a transparent manner which means you can go online and see on a day-by-day basis how much money you're earning from a particular song. Other publishers who do not do transparent accounting do paper accounting and they generally do it twice a year. Following the end of that half year you will receive a royalty statement showing what money has been received and from which song. Royalty income is coming in from all over the place it's not just coming from the United Kingdom, it's coming in from France, Japan and all over the world so there will be time lags.

Now each of these performing rights organizations negotiate a separate fee for each place where music will be performed publicly so things vary depending on the number of songs that are played. For example a bar which plays lounge music from 8 p.m to midnight would pay less than an elevator which plays music twenty four hours a day. In addition the size of the audience affects the fee. For example a large commercial radio station will pay more than a college radio station.

## Percentage Splits

Publishing money always gets split between the publisher and yourself. If you own your publishing the way it works is that for every dollar earned half goes to the writer and the other half to the publisher. Now if there are two writers then they split the share. If those two writers have their own publishing company but both have a publishing deal with a different publishing company then it would get split down half again.

The minimum percentage split these days for a brand-new songwriter is going to be 75/25 in favor of the songwriter. The more successful the songwriter the larger their share becomes since there's likely going to be a bidding war for them. The money splits into two forms. There are what are called advances and there are what are called royalty shares or royalties. Let's deal with the royalties first because they tie back into those three sources of publishing income that we talked about earlier.

Now let's assume that we are doing a 75/25 deal here on performance income. The income is going to be collected by one of the performing rights organizations and their sister organizations around the world. Their rules say that the writer must be paid at least fifty percent of income. Assuming that you've done a 75/25 deal with the publisher they are then going to pay you a half of the income from the performing rights organization and retain their twenty five percent. In addition to your own recording of your own song the publisher may find other song other writers to record the same song and then increase the income stream of that song. In that case the publisher might say they have done more work and so are entitled to a larger share than twenty five percent. There are also ways in which the royalty share to the writer increases and that is typically done on a time or a success basis. For example the royalty share which we said was 75/25 may apply for the initial contract period. Suppose the artists reaches the last option period you can assume that they have a really large career at this point. Then they might expect 85/15 for songs written during the fifth and final period of this contract and that's called a royalty escalation. Those royalties always apply to the period during which the song is written. So any songs written during the first contract period are always going to be a 75/25. That's not going to change but anything written under a different period of conditions will apply to that particular period.

# **Streaming Royalties**

Streaming has really taken over as the main way to listen to music and it's continuing to grow. Spotify is the main player in this arena. Their business model pays music creators by way of the record companies and publishers who license their recordings for streaming. This amounts to about seventy percent of their revenue that they generate from selling advertising and from their subscriptions.

Spotify are continuing to increase the number of paid subscribers for their services which is creating a situation where they are making more money. However it is difficult for them to become profitable on the thirty percent of profits that they are left with. The margin just isn't big enough so what they have decided to do and just did recently was to renegotiate their agreements with all of the major record labels. Previously the record labels used to get about fifty eight percent of the profits because from that seventy percent we talked about twelve percent of that will go to the publishers. That fifty eight percent would go to the record companies to license the recordings for the streaming service.

Spotify decided to renegotiate all of their agreements with the major major record labels and even the association of independent labels. Effectively they reduced those payments from about fifty eight percent down to almost fifty two percent. Some of the labels have agreed and Spotify has agreed that the more subscribers they get the more that royalty rates will come up. Then in turn the more money they're going to make which is a very interesting development.

Another interesting development is that Spotify is finding that there are many independent artists who feel that they can do direct deals with. Then they may not have to pay that fifty two or fifty eight percent to the major labels demanding it. There are some independent artists that they can make a deal directly with. In that regard they could possibly pay those artists less but in turn the artist also gets more than they would through a label. If the artist is signed to a major label the major label is making fifty eight percent of the revenue. Then from that they're paying their artists on the artist's royalty rate of fifteen percent. Spotify feels that they can go directly to the artist and have them license their recordings to them. Then they could pay the artists upto forty percent directly to them which is a win win situation for Spotify and the artist. Spotify has done that on occasion although they don't want to create any problems with the major labels. At the moment they are not yet doing that on on a broad level but if your an independent artist that may not be interested in signing with a major label it might be beneficial to you.

## Cost Per Stream

Back in the day if you sold one single it would be the equivalent to one hundred and fifty streams. If you sold an album it would be the equivalent to one thousand five hundred streams. In RIAA (Recording Industry Association of America) terms Gold is seven hundred and fifty million streams and Platinum is one point five billion streams. All streams are considered equal which means it doesn't matter whether that stream comes from Spotify, YouTube or Google.

In 2015 there was a study done which calculated how many streams it would take to receive a monthly minimum wage of twelve hundred and sixty dollars. The way they came up with the numbers was basically taking what each major streaming service paid out per play. Then using that number to figure out how many streams would be needed to bring you to twelve hundred and sixty dollars a month. For reference that is for independent artists.

## Google Play

Has over one billion active users and pays out 0.0073 cents per play to artists. In that case an artist would need about one hundred and seventy two thousand plays to earn the minimum wage.

## Tidal

Has over three million active users in fifty three countries and pays out 0.0070 per play. In that case an artist would need about one hundred and seventy two thousand plays to earn the minimum wage.

## YouTube

Almost five billion videos are watched everyday on YouTube. However they pay the lowest amount at 0.0003 per play and to reach the minimum wage amount it would require four point two million plays.

## Napster

Reported over four million active users and pay the most at 0.0167 per play. However the platform does not have many active users and so it might be difficult to scale. For a minimum wage you would need ninety thousand plays on the platform which is easy to achieve.

## Deezer

Available in over one hundred and eighty countries with more than forty million licensed tracks pays out 0.0056 cents per stream. To reach the minimum wage number would require at least two hundred and sixty thousand plays.

## Spotify

Almost one hundred million paid subscribers. While the service has the highest number of paid subscriptions artists often complain about the low payouts. Spotify pays out only point 0.0038 per stream and that means you would need three hundred and eighty thousand plays to reach the minimum wage amount.

## **Estimates**

The listed price per plays can vary based off of a number of factors such as, was the person that played a paid member or were they a free member when they listened to it? What ads were being played? What country was it played in? No stream is built the same, you may see consistency over the course of a couple weeks but the following week it could completely change. For example during Super Bowl week that price could go up or down depending on advertising. It has all sorts of things to do with algorithms that the streaming companies have put together to determine. Fundamentally there is no consistency or exact number, you can only get close to it.

How are you enjoying this book so far? I would love to hear back from you in the reviews section. Please leave a great honest review on Amazon, Thanks!

# Licensing and Sampling

# **Licensing an Overview**

Music licensing is an over four billion dollar worth industry with a huge ongoing need for new music. Maybe you've heard about it before but you pictured it as somebody sitting in front of a piano coming up with a cheesy jingle for a commercial. However nowadays it's a little bit different. Artists are creating modern music in any style that you can think of. Then they are getting it placed on popular TV shows, movies and commercials. It can then be a great way to gain massive exposure on an international level. Say you get a major placement in a blockbuster movie or something big that gets a lot of eyeballs and media attention on it. Your artist career is directly tied to that success and you can generate an instant buzz. Then as a result you can command bigger fees for your music. Many well known artists got their big break from TV placements. Snow Patrol had the Grey's Anatomy placements and Imagine Dragons had their song covered on Glee after which the song blew up.

Not only fame wise but financially it can be lucrative. Music licensing is one of the few businesses where you can get paid over and over again for the same work. For example every time a TV show airs you are getting paid. When it for years and years it ends up earning you huge royalties. In addition if that show gets aired in another country it's going to be even more lucrative.

## **Music Licensing Definition**

Music licensing defined is the process of acquiring the rights to use music from the copyright holder in exchange for a fee. There are many things to consider in the process and it can become quite complex since it depends on numerous factors. If you are the rights holder you need to consider what licenses you will need, style of music you require, the application(s) for the music, duration you need the music for, distribution area and location of the copyright owner. For simplicity's sake whenever you create a production using music, be sure to acquire all necessary licenses and clear all the rights. The more licenses you need and the more organisations you need to contact, the more time and money you are going to need.

## Content Producer

Anybody who's creating audio-visual content such as a TV shows, movies, commercials or anything like that is a content producer. That could also be a radio station, a network or a movie production company. Music is the best way to motivate and change people's minds. For example if you play a very sad song to somebody their mood will be altered by that. Content producers know that and so that's why they will pay very generously for music.

## Music Libraries

Music libraries serve the requirements of content producers by offering them a library of music to choose from. To enable a content producer to easily find exactly the kind of music they want they encode metadata onto every single track in the library. The content producer can then quickly type in some tags and find songs that fit their narrative. For example if they need an uplifting pop song well the music library will have a whole series of tracks with metadata on that have words like inspirational, uplifting, EDM and so on.

## Copyright Owner

Copyright owners are the composers who provide music to the libraries. If you can serve the requirements of a music library you're going to do much better than anybody else. The best thing about music licensing is it will actually push you to make music you probably wouldn't have thought about doing on your own. Building a large catalogue of music and being able to consistently produce good music is the key to succeed.

## Licenses

In the music licensing world there are four types of licenses. Synchronisation Licenses, Master Recording Licenses, Mechanical Licenses and Performance Licenses.

## Synchronisation License

This is the permission to synchronize music with a visual sequence such as on TV, in a movie, documentary, commercial and so on. Granted by the copyright holder.

## Master Recording License

This is the permission to use the original sound recording and is granted by the copyright holder.

## Mechanical License

If a content producer wants to copy music then they will require a mechanical license. This will allow them to make CD's, DVD's or other physical products such as toys or USB drives. Digital downloads also require a mechanical license. Granted by the copyright holder.

## Performance License

Permission granted by the copyright holder to broadcast music in public. Required whenever music is used on radio, TV, shops, restaurants and any other public places. In addition you will require a performance license for using music online. For example online movies or website players.

*In music licensing there are three types of music available. Those are stock music, custom music and hit music.*

## **Popular Music**

Popular (hit) music is familiar to the public and that is obviously an advantage to using it. The disadvantage is it is expensive and difficult to license. In order to use it you will require: a sync license issued by a publisher, a master license issued by a record label, a mechanical license and a performance license issued by a performance rights organisation. Sometimes you may acquire a sync license from a publisher, but without a master license from the record label. Also the cost for a master license could be over your intended budget. In these situations you can cover the song and then you don't need any other licenses. In fact this is commonplace when using hit music.

## **Stock Music**

Stock music will always include all licenses because it is designed for use with films, TV and other productions. Since the publisher is also the copyright holder things get much less complicated and cheaper. There are two types of stock music, royalty free and non-royalty free. Royalty free stock music requires you to pay once and allows you to use that music indefinitely. On the other hand for every copy you make and for every medium you use non royalty free music in you are required to pay. This is paid possibly for every year which you use that music. When using stock music, you will need a sync license, master license and a performance license from the publisher or a sync licensing agent.

## **Custom Music**

Should your budget allow it custom music is the best choice because the music is created specifically your production. It will require a larger budget but don't forget it will save you time and money long term because you don't have to find or edit the music. Ultimately with higher quality music your productions will improve which will in turn result in more income. With custom music you will need: a sync license, a master license and a mechanical license.

## Video Games

Video games are another area that's extremely beneficial to music. In a game they need background music like almost like for a movie. Grand Theft Auto was one of the first games to use a lot of music. They basically had radio stations of every single genre and used popular music. The video game market is huge so it will be nice to get your music placed in a game. There's different kinds of music for games depending on the genre. There's the kind where the game developer will license music from major artists and then there's those using custom royalty free music.

The video game area is not a royalty producing area. In most cases it's a flat fee type of situation and in those type of negotiations you should get the best fee possible without wrecking the deal. Not too much but not too little. The other thing about video licenses is they are not like a TV or a motion picture license where the licenses is for life. In video games the standard is a seven to ten year license.

## **Get Connected**

Getting your music onto commercials, video games, movies and stuff like is not as hard as you think. What you really have to do is put yourself out there and think outside the box. Music supervisors are listed all over the internet and you can reach them through social media. Find the names of music supervisors for films, TV shows and networks. Send them your music. You could also reach out to local companies and businesses and offer to make them commercials and advertisements.

Networking is one of the biggest tools that we are likely underutilizing. If you're not getting placements then you need to be networking more. Hang out in the studios where major artists are coming through and recording. Then there's all these expos, festivals and conventions. These are all places that you need to go to meet the right people. Work your way around and talk to these people. Bring business cards, USB drives of music or whatever. It's not just like a magical thing where all you do is send your music out and then you get paid. Keep in mind it's difficult but start low and work your way up. If you're determined to do it then invest in yourself instead of sitting at home wondering how to get your music out there.

# **Sampling**

The definition of sampling is to copy an element from a song and use it in another song. That could be a vocal, melody or section of a particular song. It is really based on an old idea of taking from something that previously existed and honoring it in a new way. The hip hop scene pioneered the art of sampling. Back in the early days most producers would sample records without asking for permission. The foundations of hip hop were built on that. However some rights holders didn't agree to their recordings being sampled and decided they have the right to control what can and cannot be done with them.

When you sample from a sound recording you are generally taking two copyrights. Those are the copyright in the sound recording and then within that sound recording is someone's composition. Ideally you require permission to use that from both the songwriter and publisher of that song. Technically as the songwriter or publisher you have the right to exclude others from using it. Without receiving permission to use a sample you will be liable for legal action.

## How To Clear Samples

If you want to use samples in your music then you will need clearance and that really is upto the preference of the copyright owner. If they don't like what you did with their song then they might stop you from sampling it. However if they give you clearance then you will have to pay up front, acquire a Mechanical License and then pay a percentage of royalties from any income. Should you use that song in other ways then you may also need to apply for other licenses such as a performance license. Your publisher should take care of all that for you.

The more famous the songs are or the more you use of them then the more you have to pay to clear them. This is important because based upon how much of that sample you use you will have to share more or less percentage of your revenue share. If you use up to two seconds you share two percent, if you use upto fifteen seconds you share ten percent and if you use up to sixty seconds you share twenty percent.

The next thing step is to register your song with a performance rights organization such as ASCAP or BMI. This is so they can keep track of the money that needs to be distributed out. Then that basically gives you the rights to put the song out there. With that all cleared you can sell the song and as it becomes more popular you will get your money back whilst the copyright holder will receive their percentage.

# Distribution and Merchandising

# **Distribution**

Distribution is a term used as far as getting music to retail either physically or digitally through a distribution company. Historically distributors are the people who actually work with the warehouses and get CDs out to retail stores. They will have customer service representatives working with different outlets such as Walmart, Target or any retailers that sell music. Nowadays their main focus is to work with digital outlets such as iTunes, Spotify and all of the digital streaming or sales platforms. Typically a distribution company is in-house at a record label. In cases where record labels or sometimes artists don't have distribution they will sign a contract with another label to use their distributors.

When you have music ready and you want to put it online for sale you are going to need a distributor. After all you've gone through all the hard work of writing great songs and you do that to either find your fan base or supply them with new content. If you are signed to a record label then usually they will take care of that for you. Otherwise there are two main digital distribution options out there, Tunecore and Distrokid. Let's take a look at the comparisons between the two.

## **Tunecore**

TuneCore came to the market and it allowed independent artists to upload their music to the various platforms for a one-time upfront fee and then keep all of the sales revenue. That was groundbreaking and they've since gone on to offer a lot of other services.

Tunecore allows you to upload an album for thirty dollars for the first year and then its fifty dollars for each following year after that. For a single you're looking at ten dollars per year.

As mentioned, one of the reasons for its popularity is because you get to keep one hundred percent of the profits after you've paid them to upload that album, single or ringtone. All of that money comes back to you. Now that's really cool because in most distribution situations the store and then the distributor take a percentage of those sales. In a major distribution deal sometimes the labels are only getting sixty percent of sales revenue.

Bottom line is if you want to get your music out there on the major marketplaces then Tunecore is a great option for that. They are certainly the biggest in the marketplace. Included in their service are daily sales and trend reports. Those are really useful because you need to know how many units you're selling, where you're selling them and how many streams you're getting. All that information is very important and you get that whenever you upload your content. In addition they can even help you design album artwork plus various other services.

Check it out for yourself visit https://www.tunecore.com

## **Distrokid**

Distrokid is fairly new to the marketplace but a lot of major independent artists are starting to gravitate over to it. With Distrokid you pay only twenty dollars to upload unlimited albums and songs for a complete year. That's right TuneCore and others charge every year for each project but with Distrokid you can upload as much content as you want for one fee a year. Distrokid wins the pricing battle here because you can either pay TuneCore twenty dollars for the first year and then fifty dollars for every year after that. Alternatively with Distrokid all you have to pay is twenty dollars a year and you can upload as many singles or as many full albums as you want. There are no restrictions on that.

Another great feature about Distrokid is that they tend to get their content onto the digital platforms much faster than other digital distributors. I've actually uploaded an EP, made it live for the next day and it was there in all of the stores simultaneously at the same time within three days. The one thing you want to do when your music comes out is to be able to get on social media and send people where you want them to buy or stream your music. At that time you want it to be there, you don't want to have to structure your marketing plan to think okay well it is live on iTunes but it's not on Amazon so we can't use that that link yet. Then you can have that confidence knowing that your product is going to be live in all those different stores and streaming outlets at the same time. I found with Distrokid that actually happens more often than TuneCore or some of the other online distributors. In addition, they also provide all of the revenue and one hundred percent of the sales come back to you.

Another great thing is they will allow you to go in and create collaboration projects. For example say you have a project and there are multiple people involved in sharing the revenue of that project. Maybe another producer or songwriters that have an ownership stake in the sales. You can easily go in and create that party and then allocate any percentage of the sales to that person. All you need is their email address and what happens is when you sell one copy it will allocate the percentage of what you set and send it to them via their email address. This is a really unique and amazing structure that allows you to keep track of how much you owe everybody that has an ownership stake.

Check it out for yourself visit www.distrokid.com

## **Level Music (Free Distribution)**

Level Music is the new digital distributor on the block. Owned by The Warner Music Group it is aimed at upcoming independent artists and bands looking to distribute their music online. Right now it's in its beta version and they are allowing artists to sign up and upload for free. That means there's no fees to upload anything and you get to keep one hundred percent of your royalties which can then be sent to your PayPal account. This is an unusual move for the major record label but speculation might be that it is an A&R way for them to see how independent artists and bands are doing. Then maybe approach them and sign them if they're doing really well. Eventually they will charge some kind of fee down later on for uploads and so on but they didn't say exactly when. However they do say that they will keep everyone updated on when they will.

Distribution through Level Up allows artists to release music on all the major outlets like Google, iTunes,

Amazon, Spotify and pretty much every other digital outlet. When you sign up they give a artists and/or your band landing page. This will features links on it to their preferred music sites along with bio, pictures and so on. Fans can then visit that page to check out their favorite artist and then click the links to listen to their music. Which is a great promotional tool. In addition they also offer detailed track analysis allowing you to see where your music is being streamed and or downloaded. This is a powerful information source to help you zone in on the appropriate regions and demographics of your fans.

If you haven't found or decided on a distributor yet for your music you might want to take advantage of Level Music. Check it out to see if it might be something for you especially since it's free at the moment.

Check it out for yourself visit
https://beta.levelmusic.com/

# **Merchandising**

Music sales have fallen dramatically in the last few years. This requires a new way of thinking in order to make a great living doing what we love. Instead of trying to monetize our music we must simply get it out there for everyone to hear and then in turn become a fan of. Simply put, use it as a vehicle to build up your audience and then look at ways to monetize that. Once you have a big enough fan base merchandising is a great way to engage and build your fanbase whilst making some decent money. Take a look at some of the big YouTubers and famous bands. They earn a lot of money off their merchandise which is why they're constantly promoting and selling it. Although most artists have this issue with selling that it's so corporate and so they don't fully embrace it. But if you have a solid fan base they will buy almost anything from you. At the end of the day they love what you do and want to be seen as part of your tribe. Your main challenge is to make really creative, interesting and stylish merchandise for them. Time after the time I hear artists saying no merchandise doesn't work for me because nobody's buying. Think about it, if you're trying to sell somebody a plain t-shirt with a tiny logo of your unknown band yes it will annoy people and nobody will like it.

## **Manufacturing Merchandise**

Making merchandise is cheap, easy and can be made up almost anywhere these days. Simply browse online and you will find tons of websites around the world. Most people buy overseas but you could even buy local. Every city has a place that will manufacture and print things. The bottom line is making money and if you get an inventory of this stuff you want to be able to sell it. You don't want for it to sit in every show with nobody buying it. Many artists try to cut costs and get the cheapest possible. But the reality with that is that most of it will stay in the packaging. Then the next album comes out and it's just old merchandise that you can't get rid of.

Consider the fans because they will know the difference between good and bad quality. First and foremost don't cut costs and secondly design stuff that people will actually want. With that mindset you are more likely to have people want to buy your merchandise, even if they're not a massive fan. For example take a look at the merchandise from bands such as Slipknot and Kiss. Back in the day almost everyone had a Slipknot hoodie. Yes, there were other bands just as good but they didn't merchandise like Slipknot did and so went largely unnoticed in comparison. Take time to get the right logo, material, designs and ultimately the right merchandise out there. Don't just create merchandise for the hell of it, build a brand of cool and quality merchandise. If you just slap something together chances are you won't get it right. No one will buy your merchandise, you will be out of pocket and with a bunch of merchandise that nobody wants.

## Where to Merchandise

Touring or online are great ways to get your merchandise into the hands of your fans. Wear your merchandise and let people know where to go if they want it. At shows have a little table set up somewhere where the crowd can access it. Put it in the best light as near to the main door as possible so that when people have to walk in or out they have to go past it. Have someone attractive run the table. They will be responsible for collecting money and at the same time have them ask for email addressed. Most people will happily give them out and that can go towards email marketing campaigns.

The next best place to offer merchandise is on your website or through social media. There are many merchandise apps that you can have as a widget or setup on a separate page of your website. A lot of YouTubers have their own shop and at the end of every video they promote it. In addition they are also usually giving away free content first to incentivise customers. Do something awesome for them and then they can do something awesome in return for you. Make it easy for people to just click straight on it and buy the merchandise. Follow the same strategy to softly promote your merchandise through social media. Should anyone happen to see it they might just really like your merchandise and click the link.

## Price Points

Consider your fans demographic. What price would they be willing to pay? What can they easily afford? Maybe they are young and can just afford a sticker or badge. Maybe they are middle aged and so something in the higher price range is affordable to them. Maybe its teenagares with their parents and they can afford the extra dollars for a hoodie and so on. When you scale up make sure that whatever you manufacture is of a decent quality that you can sell at a price that is profitable for you whilst being affordable for the fans. Factor in your costs and what it would require to make a profit that your happy with. If you're pretty big and touring nationally you can get away with higher prices. Or if your starting out you might need to give away things like stickers and badges just to bring awareness to your brand.

*Do it professionally and remember to look at it as a business.*

# **Finance**

# Finance

Finance is an often overlooked field that requires extra special attention in the music business. Very few producers, artists and musicians take the time to understand it but this is the kind of stuff that will separate the amateurs from the pros. Amateurs don't consider finance, they just want to make music and hope it all works out in the end. Professionals on the contrary take care of finances before it becomes a problem because if you're not careful you can get audited, go broke, get shut down or sued. There are a lot of things that can completely wipe out your entire career. Be smart and remember that you are running yourself as a business in this industry.

## Supporting Yourself

Investing into your craft is essential in order to operate like a business and scale up. Things such as investing in studio time, mastering, web hosting and all these things that come with business ownership. If you don't have enough money and you try to get somewhere in this game you will have a hard time. A lot of artist types tend to overlook the importance of having a financial means of supporting themselves and a means to invest into their career. You can't be out here just hoping that something is going to happen, you have to put in the work. Then you hear people talking about things like a job as a way out. However for the most part a job is a way to have the means to invest into your business as a musician.

Now if you don't have a job you better have some legal means of supporting your business until you're making one hundred percent of your money from music. Until then you will need to have a way to subsidize it. Don't allow yourself to be so wrapped up in yourself chasing a dream that your family has to suffer for it. Having a job is not a cop-out it is just smart financially. There will be sacrifices on your time but you don't have time to watch TV, hang out or waste time. Maybe you have other legal means of making money. At least with a job you can get a consistent check you can start saving some you can start putting things towards the other things that you want in life. In addition with a job you have paid leave so if you need to go to a conference or take some time off to record or whatever then you can do that.

## **Money**

Undeniably if you want to see any progress or success it's not going to happen without money. Most people have a source of income whether that be a job or some situation they have set up as a means of earning money. In some cases the problem is not making money but keeping it. Understand that until you're making a decent amount of money all you need to do is maintain. Figure out what your maintenance amount is for your bills, gas, car, rent, phone bills etc. Then make sure you've got that money there. Anything above that do not touch that and let it go towards something that's going to move you forward. You don't need luxuries, spend it on things that are going to push you forward. Such as studio time, promotional materials or websites and so on. Invest in your career and yourself.

## **Tax**

Now when you start making some money from your music you will need to be careful because you will get paid differently from the average working person. The average person gets paid every week or month and tax is deducted before they are paid. For artists it's totally different. They are responsible for paying taxes on any money that they are paid. When the tax man shows up at the end of the year a lot of artists get into trouble because they don't know how much they need to put aside for tax. Yes the dreaded thing called taxes, you must file them if you are a working band, artist or musician. Especially if you own your own label or you are an indie artist.

## **Corporation**

Before you pay taxes you need to be making enough money and be registered as a business. The best way is to form a corporation and that can be an LLC (Limited Liability Corporation) or you can be an independent contractor. Some people go all the way and become a corporation ( S corp) which is a little more money but it has some great benefits as well. Whether or not you form a corporation or become an independent contractor you will be taxed. Either way that's guaranteed and so you need to save accordingly. This is unlike getting a salary from your employer. Nobody's taking those taxes out for you and you will now be responsible for paying them. Make sure that you're not being foolish with your money and have some saved up for the tax man.

## **Company Set Up**

When you set up an LLC it's the equivalent of having a new entity. In the eyes of the IRS if that legal entity gets sued they can only take things that the corporation owns. They cannot pierce through that corporation to take any of your personal assets. That's the protection you get when you're operating a corporation. Now you do have to operate the corporation according to the laws of the IRS. If you're operating it improperly then you lose that protection. Avoid spending personal money out of your business account because you need to be operating it as a separate entity. Make sure you keep this separation and if you run it properly you get to keep that protection. Have a business credit card just for expenses so you can closely monitor it.

There are other benefits of being a business and that is you can write stuff off as a tax break. That means you can write off equipment, promotional materials, advertising and you can even write off travelling expenses as long as it's a normal thing. In addition if you want to get a loan you can get business credit from a bank. It's a lot easier to get those kind of loans when you have a business registered.

## **Paying Taxes**

Once your business name has been filed and your making money whether it be through licensing, selling music, playing shows and so on. When that reaches over five hundred dollars a year you will need to file what is called a 1099 form for MISC and independent contractors. Anybody that pays you money needs to issue you a 1099 by January 31st every single year. That means they paid you money but you don't work for them. Inside it will summarize all the money that they paid you the previous year, what you are expected to report and taxes to pay on to the IRS.

Please file your taxes otherwise it will come back to haunt you especially when you start getting bigger. Don't wait until it's too late because you might get real big and the IRS will come knocking on your door. Keep track of everything, every receipt and so on. Then if you get audited you will have all your proof there.

# Financial Statements

If you don't have a business or accounting background but you find yourself running or interested in running your own company you're going to need to learn at least the basics. Particularly this is of interest to artists who are going down the independent route with your own company set up. The first things that you should learn are basic financial statements. There are three basic financial statements and these are vitally important because they paint the financial picture of your company and help you to evaluate past performance and plan for the future.

When we look at financial statements keep in mind that this is going to be at a very basic level since we are coming at it as music artists. The financial statements that we will look at are going to be for a sole proprietor. In financial accounting there are four financial statements. The income statement, the statement of owner's equity, the balance sheet and the cash flow statement. Whenever we are making financial statements we will always start with the income statement, then the owner's equity and then finally the balance sheet.

As an example let's pretend that we have a bookkeeping company called Tom's bookkeeping. Remember that the first financial statement we need to create is the income statement. At the top of every single financial statement that we make there are going to be three things. First thing is the company name, in this case it's called Tom's bookkeeping. The next thing is going to be the statement name. The first statement we make is the income statement so write that out. The next thing that we're going to write is the date or the period of time for it. An income statement is always for a period of time so your income statement should be for the year ended and then the date today. Or for the month ended and then the date today. It all depends on what period of time you are looking at for that particular income statement. Let's assume we're looking at for the year ended. Therefore it will be an income statement for Tom's bookkeeping for the year ended.

The income statement shows two major categories of accounts, that is revenues and expenses. Accounting equation revenues are either the amount of money you charge per hour / per project or the amount you sell something for. As a whole the income statement will show revenues minus expenses to give you a final net income.

The next major category of accounting on the income statement is expenses. These are things that you have to pay for in the course of doing business. Such as your rent, utilities, employee salaries and all sorts of things like that. Again revenues minus expenses will give you the net income.

The next statement we need to make is a statement of owner's equity. Process wise the first thing to do is going to be putting a name at the top and in this case it's Tom's bookkeeping. Next you will need a statement name and in this case it's the statement of owner's equity. Then the third input is the time period or the date of the statement of owner's equity and the income statement. The period of time should look exactly the same. So in this case it would be for the year end. The statement of owner's equity always has the five same things. Number one the opening balance, two investment by owner, three net income or loss, four withdrawals by owner and five the closing balance of the capital account. We always make the statement of owner's equity second and the reason for that is because we are going to use that closing capital balance on the next statement.

Following on is the balance sheet on which there's always going to be the company's name and date. Regarding date we don't put for the period ended but rather we just look at the date that it is concerned with. The accounting equation is assets equal liabilities added to the owner's equity. That's exactly what the balance sheet is showing and that's what we try to balance. On one side will be balance then with liabilities and owner's equity on the other side. Assets have a future benefit so those are accounts like cash, office supplies, equipment. Those assets can be totalled up at the bottom. Liabilities are things owed to outsiders of the company such as accounts payable, notes payable, debt to bank and so on. For our owner's equity section we're going to go back and remember that number that we had for closing capital balance of the year ended. Write the amount and take the total of liabilities and owner's equity. If these two match meaning total assets equals total liabilities and owner's equity that means your accounting equation works and your balance sheet works. If these numbers don't match, you've made an error and you will have to review your work.

Next is the income statement, otherwise referred to as the profit and loss statement. This shows a company's profits or losses during a specific period and it highlights revenues and expenses divided into operating or non-operating income. Operating income begins with sales and costs of products sold to calculate the gross profit margin. After that it minuses operating expenses that are divided into selling expenses and admin expenses. This includes items such as advertising and commissions for sales personnel. Admin expenses include any overheads that are not a part of sales. For example, office materials and utilities. Operating income is the sum of the gross profit minus your operating expenses. After that you add or minus any non-operating income such as interest to calculate your net income.

The last financial statement to know about is the statement of cash flow. This one is really vital, many businesses have failed not based on profit but based on cash flow problems. A statement of cash flow shows a company's income and outcome of cash during a specific period. The cash flow statement consists of cash flows both from operational and investment activities. You begin with total net income and then accomodate for any non-cash expenses such as depreciation, accounts receivable or payable.

Understanding these basic three financial statements will give you a better understanding of how your company is performing financially. Then you can have a better foresight into success and financial planning for your career in the music business.

# **Crowdfunding**

If your looking to kick start a project such as an album crowdfunding is a very unique tool that we have available these days. Musicians and even labels are actually having a lot of success with it. The fact is that labels don't have that much money these days and you might be the one responsible for raising funds. Albums are expensive, there's ways of getting around that but you can only cut corners so much. The other reason you might want to do crowdfunding is that it pre funds merchandise and any other items that you actually have to go and print. If you do vinyl, t-shirts or any kind of merchandise then you have to pay up front. Coming up with the money for that can be really tough. It also involves thorough research ahead of time in order to approximate sales, distribution and accounting goals.

The great thing about crowdfunding is that it can be a part of fan involvement. Essentially it can be a massive awareness campaign and you will create thousands of new fans that you did not have before. To get started you need an audience. If you have fans who are openly asking when you are creating a new album then it could be a great time to start a campaign. In the case where your starting from ground zero don't worry because you don't need a ton of people to be successful. The main focus is to make sure you have a responsive list whatever size that is. Engage them and make them feel a part of the project. Send out a survey to gauge in terms of interest if is this something they think is a good idea and is this something they would want to participate in. If so ask them for a dollar amount of what they would be willing to contribute.

Surveying should be done regularly. You can use applications such as Google Forms, Facebook polls, Survey Monkey and so on. Put it out on social media, in your email list and as part of your marketing. Emails are great for this because they are a lot more personal.

## **Decide On The Project**

Now if you are using something like Patreon or Bandcamp where you want to have ongoing membership type things that's a different kind of crowdfunding. There are some amazing platforms out there that you can definitely use if you want to have more of an evergreen type of crowdfunding. There's a few other names out there where people can just pay you regularly to produce content which is amazing. The concept I'm talking about here is more of something with a start and end date. For example, a new album.

Decide the project for the crowdfunding campaign. Is it an EP, an album, a music video or some kind of cool concept thing that nobody has heard of before? What's the project, what stage are you at right now and how long is it going to take to finish it? Again you can ask your fanbase for their opinion.

When you have decided on a crowdfunding campaign you are going to need to set a budget. How much is it going to cost from start to finish? Factor in all of the costs from merchandise to shipping. Keep a progress report and share that budget with your fans. Keep them involved, people forget how expensive it is to make really good music. They forget how much gear costs, how much studio costs and just all the details of where money goes. Record all your costs and orders. In addition don't forget exchanging money costs and fees.

## Fan Base

Calculate how many followers and subscribers you have on social media that would support you either by contributing or sharing. When you have your total numbers you will have a good idea of where you're at. Contrast your total number of followers against the cost of the project. Then decide is this realistic if only one out of ten people donated somewhere around the average amount, what will you end up with? Don't expect your fans to pick up the entire bill because overall you want to keep it relational and not transactional.

Take care of your fans and decide on the main perks that you will offer. What do your fans want, what special items can you offer that they won't get anywhere else? Try to make things easier by offering some digital options or exclusive items during the campaign and then maybe regular items during the presale after the campaign.

Timing is everything, you've got to be decisive on the time of your launch date. Try to get as much done before it launches. For example if you have some tracks that are already mastered or mixed give little sneak peeks to get people more excited. Then as for the duration, typically thirty days is good enough. Anymore and it's going to be a long haul, so be prepared to be exhausted by the end of it. Also people will also lose interest and it'll get old so just keep that in mind.

## **Investors**

Alternative to crowdfunding you can get investors on board. There are so many investors looking to be involved in the music business. In some cases they might not care so much of the music simply they want to know what kind of success you have.

Most investors don't say "hey I'm an angel investor" because they would be bombarded with people giving them pitches. Most are not professional investors meaning they don't invest full-time. Oftentimes they are people with disposable income or wealthy professionals and successful entrepreneurs. Investing could be their hobby and they want to invest in things they haven't the time or talent for.

Finding investors is typically through informal networks. Look to people who are connectors and tell them you are looking for investment. Lawyers, accountants and so on are examples of people usually connected to investors. Start planting the seeds and spreading the word.

When you find an investor the mindset you should have when meeting with them shouldn't be what can I get out of you but to actually talk about how does my involvement help us collectively. Or how I can help you and your company or your venue or your brands? Make it more about this is what I can do for you.

Show that you're already able to make some kind of impact because people are purchasing your music and your generating a buzz. Investors need to believe in you and see the proof of it.

*If you have those things going for you then you have value already.*

# **Sponsorship**

Sponsorship is a concept involving a company supporting an artist through funding or providing merchandise and or services to them. This is in return for the artist representing them and advertising that particular company. Whether it be banners at the back of a show or the artists wearing company clothes in public or on social media. Every agreement will be different and you need to be aware of the requirements. Essentially it's about aligning businesses and artists to benefit from the mutual association of each other.

This will give you exposure in places that you might not have before. Companies will take out magazine adverts, post banners on forums, have their own social media marketing and so on. Offering your face and likeness for them to promote works really well because it introduces you to a whole new market that you might not of had access to previously. Plus financially you are receiving some sort of discount or help with the cost of business. Maybe you can save on guitar strings, cables, clothing and so on. All of this can be financially beneficial.

Now you might be under the wrong impression that sponsorship simply means free stuff. Indeed there might be some people out there who get free stuff, such as a mega rockstar who could get any guitar shipped to any country any day of the week at no cost. But understand this is not the norm, it's a special circumstance because they are of such a high stature. Your everyday working professional doesn't get that kind of treatment.

## How to Get Sponsored

As an artist there are many different companies you could be sponsored by. However you will need a fan base because if you're just the average artist doing opening shows then it doesn't offer a company much value. Companies are looking for artists who can give them more exposure. If you have a decent sized fan base than they will either approach you or you can pitch to them. Before you work with a company consider if they fit your music style. Don't go after a company that you think you need to be a part of because someone else is. If you never use their stuff or if your not a big fan of their don't do it because you will get trapped with a company that you don't like. For example maybe you sign with a company that is doing unethical business and now you have that association. Make sure you like the company and believe in what they're doing. Those are the most important things that you need to consider. It's a good idea to really zone in on exactly the kind of companies you want to work with. Maybe it's clothing brands or music equipment. Think of what you want or what you regularly use. It all comes down to what you are looking for. Maybe it's money or because you want to play their guitars?

## **Offer Value**

If they haven't approached you, call the company and ask who you need to speak to about sponsorships. You can pitch to the people on the phone, arrange a meeting or start an email chain. In the case where you are a bigger artist the company will want to meet you in person or if your a little lesser-known they might just talk to you over the phone. Be professional towards these people and be on time. Tell them what you can do for them and how they will benefit from working with you. There's all kinds of things you could do with sponsorships so don't be afraid to ask. Discuss it and be professional.

Why does a company need you? Number one is legitimacy and reputation. Again the association of business and artist together makes both look better. For example if a guitar player is not only a great player but he's got a bunch of hits the chances are this company wants to work with them. That helps them target customers because they are likely to be fans of the artist and follow what they do or use. Chances are you saw your artists using a piece of equipment and it influenced you to buy it.

You will probably get turned down a lot but eventually you might get a yes. Just remember you need some sort of fan following because they're not just going to sponsor you if you have nothing going on. Have set up a digital press kit with all your stats and materials. Highlight if you have a high social media following or lots of likes and engagement. They will want to know things such as. Do you have music on iTunes? A YouTube channel with lots of views? Ultimately they want to be associated with any business that is doing well. Incidentally it has less to do with how good you are at music but more about how profitable you can be.

# **Conclusion**

# **Time, Money and Age**

The time money ratio is the way you can calculate what you should be doing yourself and what you should be paying people to do. Time management is where you discover the time and money ratio. Both are incredibly valuable assets and you have decide how to value them. On one side of paper write down what's you're best at and on the other side write down what it takes you the longest to do. It's not necessarily what you are the worst at. For instance let's say your a music producer and you make music all day. How long does the process take? Do you spend hours mixing, mastering and getting it ready? Or does it take the longest to do the graphic design stuff? What are you best at? Focus on what you are really good at. Then write down your time obligations whether it be a job, family, college, school, etc. Write down what your priorities are and what you absolutely have to get done.

Now you need to establish what you feel your time is worth because when we go to a day job or trade time for money that's really what the hourly rate is. On a piece of paper write down what you think your hourly rate is worth. As an example if you value yourself at fifteen dollars an hour and you work for four hours then the price is obviously sixty dollars. You could spend that four hours doing some graphic design or you could hire a professional graphic designer to do it for thirty dollars. If you don't have the time or experience, spend the money and get it done professionally.

Prioritize your time. Think about how much time you waste. Log down all the time you spend in a week and look to trim the fat. If you spent as much time working on your music and marketing as you do on social media you could be one of the biggest names in the game. Let's say you spend an hour on social media every day. Your posting on Instagram, Facebook, networking on LinkedIn or whatever. If you sign up for a service such as HootSuite it can schedule your social media. Spend a few hours on one day getting all your social media posts done for the week. That helps you schedule your social posts to free up time and then you don't need to be checking all the time.

Now a lot of you guys don't want to spend money on these things because you don't believe in yourself enough to invest in yourself. Understand that your time is an investment and it is the most valuable asset in your life. Start looking at all these different services that can help you get to where you need to be a little bit faster and make your life so much easier. Look at where you're spending your money and time. Figure out how you can give more money and time to the things that really matter in your career. Maybe you want to spend a couple dollars once a month and have a graphic designer create some content or maybe you find someone with a camera to shoot you a basic video. It all boils down to either you have the time or the money to pay somebody else who has the time to do it for you.

*Hopefully one day this time can turn into money so the time that you do have will be enjoyed with your friends and family living your best life.*

## **Time is Running Out**

Slowly but surely are we running out of time. Many of us in the music business are concerned about age. Did we miss the boat, am I too old to make it? It really depends on your strengths and belief in yourself, then combine that with how hard are you willing to work.

You are never too old to make it in the music business. When somebody buys music they don't buy it because of your age. In fact a lot of times people don't know how old you are. Incidentally you get better with age and your music gets better. Producing and songwriting take a lot of skill, networking and brand building. That doesn't happen in a year or even in five years.

There is a side of the music industry that's toxic in this regard. They look for the youngest talent because they can exploit them. Day after day you see these young artists getting screwed over on deals. Look at Justin Bieber, he got discovered when he was really young. Do you want to be that person? Is that your dream to get signed at a young age with a huge cash payment that you are in debt to. Now every deal is different obviously but what I'm getting at is that when you get a little bit older and know your value you can make better decisions.

Alternatively there are lots of other things you can do if you feel limited by age. You don't necessarily have to be the face of it. Have you ever thought about songwriting for other people? Maybe you're not a singer yourself but you love to write. There are so many songwriters out there that are in their seventies with dozens of number-one hits. The music industry is endless when it comes to capabilities and potential. Have you ever thought about licensing your music? You can always get your music on TV, commercials and films. There are some pretty massive license deals out there.

At the end of the day don't worry about how old you are worry about your music worry and your fanbase. Understand your audience. For example if if you are a country music singer your audience age range is going to be different than if your making top forty music. You need to be able to relate to them and be relevant. First of all make music for yourself so whoever you are technically is your target audience.

## **The Exit**

If you make music full-time you need to understand what your exit strategy is or what your overall goal is. If you're a music producer or artists you can't possibly think that you will be making one style forever. Tastes evolve and people change regardless of if it is making boat loads of money. Music making is an art and it should be about the love of it and if you can make some money while you're doing it even better. When you get older you might want to do something else.

Focus on what you want to do. If you spend any energy listening to those people that don't believe in you and are telling you what to do then those people aren't really supporting you. Sit-down with them and tell them making music makes me feel fulfilled and making music is all that I ever want to do in life. I'm a much happier person when I'm not muffled and boxed in by everybody telling me that my dream is stupid.

*We all have our ups and downs, adversity and obstacles but it's up to us to get past that. It's up to us to make sure that little spark inside of us keeps burning.*

## Are You Ready To Start Earning REAL INCOME With Your Music?

https://www.subscribepage.com/musicbiz

# Thanks for Reading!

*What did you think of:*

**Music Business Skills For Musicians: Make Money from Music, Discover The Music Industry and Explode Your Music Career!**

I know you could have picked any number of books to read, but you picked this book and for that I am extremely grateful.

I hope that it added at value and quality to your everyday life. If so, it would be really nice if you could share this book with your friends and family by posting to Facebook and Twitter.

If you enjoyed this book and found some benefit in reading this, I'd like to hear from you and hope that you could take some time to post a review. Your feedback and support will help this author to greatly improve his writing craft for future projects and make this book even better.

I want you, the reader, to know that your review is very important and so, if you'd like to leave a review, all you have to do is click here and away you go. I wish you all the best in your future success!

Also check out my other books:

https://www.amazon.com/Tommy-Swindali/e/B01CBD9PRW

Thank you and good luck!

*Tommy Swindali*
*2019*

Printed in Great Britain
by Amazon